Rawdon Briggs Lee

A history and description of the collie or sheep dog in his British varieties

Rawdon Briggs Lee

**A history and description of the collie or sheep dog in his British varieties**

ISBN/EAN: 9783337203290

Printed in Europe, USA, Canada, Australia, Japan

Cover: Foto ©ninafisch / pixelio.de

More available books at **www.hansebooks.com**

A

# HISTORY AND DESCRIPTION

OF THE

# COLLIE or SHEEP DOG

IN

## HIS BRITISH VARIETIES.

BY

### RAWDON LEE,

AUTHOR OF "THE FOX TERRIER;" KENNEL EDITOR OF
"THE FIELD."

The Illustrations by Arthur Wardle.

LONDON:
HORACE COX,
"THE FIELD" OFFICE, 346, STRAND, W.C.

1890.

LONDON:
PRINTED BY HORACE COX, 346, STRAND, W.C.

GIFT OF

# PREFACE.

LONG ago admirers of the collie pronounced him the most useful and the most intelligent of all dogs. At the present time he still bears that fair fame, and, in addition thereto, occupies a position second to none of the canine race in pecuniary value. Hundreds of pounds are often given for the best specimens, so he is cared for accordingly. Fifty years since, and before the establishment of dog shows, a five pound note was fair value for the best working animal that could be produced; now he will bring more than twenty times that sum for his good looks alone. The latter have made him a favourite, and his popularity is only excelled by that of the fox terrier.

Much has been written about the sheep dog or collie, and no doubt abundance of information thereon is ready to follow. In the following pages an endeavour has been made to trace his progress from the fold and mountain to the drawing room and the parlour, not omitting to specially mention all the varied duties he is now called upon and expected to fulfil.

The subject of competitive trials has had particular

attention, and my knowledge of such contests has enabled me to treat them more fully than any previous writer. If my praise of "Collie trials with sheep" has any effect in extending such useful institutions to some locality in which they have not previously been known, a good object will have been served; for the shepherd applies to his dog the motto, "handsome is that handsome does." The more sensible the dog, the better his adaptability for household usefulness and as an ordinary companion. Dog shows have added to the beauty of the collie; the trials must add to his intelligence.

As in my preceding volume on the Fox Terrier, appropriate vignettes are introduced, which, with the full-page wood engravings of celebrities in the sheep dog world, are the work of Mr. Arthur Wardle. Both he and the engraver, Mr. C. Butterworth, have done the portion of the task set them satisfactorily.

RAWDON LEE.

BRIXTON, LONDON,
*June*, 1890.

# CONTENTS.

|  | PAGE. |
|---|---|
| Preface | iii |

### CHAPTER I.
Early History—Varieties of the Shepherd's Dog—Scriptural Allusion—Aldrovandus—An Early Recipe for Dyeing a Dog—Supposed Origin—Alleged Crosses ... ... 1

### CHAPTER II.
The Collie—The Meaning of the Word—The "Sportsman's Cabinet"—Tail Cutting—North Country Collies—In Literature and Art—His Character—Work and Show ... ... 20

### CHAPTER III.
Early Shows—The First Classes for Sheep Dogs—The Winners therein—Great Dogs, "Cockie," "Charlemagne," "Rutland," &c.—Notable Kennels—High Prices ... 42

### CHAPTER IV.
The Smooth-coated Collie—What He Springs from—His Varieties and Types—His Colours—Some of the best Dogs—A Sagacious Bitch—Punishment of a Dog Thief ... 70

## CHAPTER V.

The Old English "Bob-tailed" Sheep Dog—His Origin—Reinagle's Illustration in the "Sportsman's Cabinet"—Richardson's Description—"Idstone"—Early Classes—Dr. Edwardes-Ker's Opinion—Description and Standard of Points    80

## CHAPTER VI.

Trials with Sheep—The First Meeting—Chief Gatherings—North of England and Wales—The Queen Present—A Typical Trial—Description of some Competing Dogs—Rules, Regulations, and General Management    ... 101

## CHAPTER VII.

The Collie Clubs—Their Standard of Excellence—Scales and Points—The Scottish Collie Club—Intelligence of the Collie—Some Anecdotes—Trained to Perform—Sheep Worrying...    ... 121

## CHAPTER VIII.

Management—Rearing Puppies—Food—Bedding—Some Ailments and Disorders—Preparing for Show—Conclusion    ... ... ... 136

## ADDENDA.

The Collie Clubs: Their Rules and Regulations    ... 149

# ILLUSTRATIONS.

| | |
|---|---:|
| "OLD COCKIE" AND "CHARLEMAGNE" ... | *Frontispiece* |
| A GOOD HEAD—METCHLEY WONDER'S. (Vignette)... | viii |
| "OF THE PYRENEAN TYPE." (Vignette.) ... | 20 |
| "LOST AND FOUND." (Vignette.) | 41 |
| "METCHLEY WONDER" AND "GREAT ALNE DOUGLAS" (rough-coated modern winners) | 66 |
| "ON THE HILL SIDE." (Vignette.) | 69 |
| "HERDWICK HERDSMAN" AND "HERDWICK EVA" (smooth-coated collies) ... ... | 73 |
| "HE WON'T BUDGE AN INCH." (Vignette.) | 79 |
| "SIR CAVENDISH" (old English sheepdog) | 93 |
| "NOT JUDGED YET." (Vignette.) ... | 100 |
| "THE END OF HIS TRIAL, SAFELY PENNED." (Vignette.) | 120 |
| "LOOK AT HIM NOW, SIR!" (Vignette.) ... | 135 |
| "PLEASANT DREAMS." (Vignette.) ... ... | 148 |

# THE COLLIE OR SHEEP DOG.

## CHAPTER I.

EARLY HISTORY—VARIETIES OF THE SHEPHERD'S DOG—SCRIPTURAL ALLUSION—ALDROVANDUS—AN EARLY RECIPE FOR DYEING A DOG—SUPPOSED ORIGIN—ALLEGED CROSSES.

UNLIKE many varieties of the dog common to the British Isles, and which must in a great measure be considered indigenous thereto, the shepherd's dog, in one form or another, is to be found in each hemisphere, and in every country where sheep or goats or cattle form a part of the wealth of the inhabitants, whose lives are consequently more or less pastoral. Thus, for its history we must go back many hundreds of years—so far, indeed, that particulars of its origin appear to be entirely lost.

Many eminent naturalists, Buffon amongst the number, were of opinion that the original dog was a sheep dog, or one which answered the same purpose: an animal sagacious enough to assist the shepherd to watch the flocks and herds; strong enough to protect them from ravenous animals, and ferocious enough to keep the thief and the robber at a distance. Thus, in those countries where wild animals were powerful and numerous, the shepherds' dogs were and are big and strong in proportion; whilst here, following the extinction of the wolf, the sheep dogs gradually came to lose their ferocity; and nature, as usual, producing the fittest for the purpose, gave us the sagacious and handsome creature which, in a somewhat improved form, survives at the present time. The huge dogs of Thibet, more mastiff-like in appearance than anything else, form a connecting link between the modern sheep dog and his historic ancestor, when the latter was expected to perform the treble duty already mentioned as required of him. And many of the wandering, pastoral tribes in parts of Asia and elsewhere, have their shepherds' dogs as big and strong and ferocious as they can be made. Much of their sagacity is thus lost; and even where the flocks form the chief wealth of the country, we look in vain for that almost human knowledge and extraordinary instinct found in the common sheep dog of the British Isles.

More frequently seen in this country than are those of Thibet, we find the so-called Pyrenean sheep dogs which from time to time appear at our leading dog shows. Here again have we a large, powerful, and handsome animal with sufficient strength, if he possesses the courage, to successfully cope with any wolf that may feel inclined to pick off one of his master's sheep. The Pyrenean dog, like his cousin of Thibet, is produced of the character best fitted to be useful to the shepherd on his native mountains. This dog not only is required to prevent the flock from becoming scattered, but to guard it from the depredations of wolves and foxes, which are by no means uncommon. The Pyrenean sheep (or guard) dogs seen here are probably about 8olb. or over in weight, mostly white in colour, with fawn or pale brown markings, very much in appearance resembling what would be produced from a cross between a Scotch collie as we see him now and a modern St. Bernard. He is light in colour and sagacious in expression; whilst the Asiatic dog used for very much similar purposes is dark in colour, black and tan, and ferocious in appearance. These two varieties are mentioned thus early in order to draw attention to the fact that such dogs do exist, and to a certain extent are used in the protection of the flocks and herds; but, personally, I do not believe that they have any right to be classified amongst the sheep dogs proper. Then there are the herd dogs of the Himalayas, again strong, ferocious animals, guardians of the flocks and herds of their owners; and most countries have bred at one time or another similar animals, from which the common stock has evidently descended.

Both Homer and Virgil make repeated allusions to dogs of various descriptions, those of the swineherds being perhaps the nearest approach to the shepherds' dogs. They are sometimes called savage dogs, at other times mastiffs.

> Nor, last forget thy faithful dogs: but feed
> With fattening whey the mastiff's generous breed,
> And Spartan race, who, for the fold's relief,
> Will prosecute with cries the nightly thief,
> Repulse the prowling wolf, and hold at bay
> The mountain robbers rushing to their prey.

Briton Riviere, R.A., one of the great animal painters of modern times, has recently given us, in a charming picture, "Pallas Athene and the Herdsman's Dogs," his suggestion of the pastoral dogs in use when Homer wrote. These are the usual hyena-wolf-like animals of the East, with erect ears and arched backs; but Riviere depicts them as better fed, healthier-looking creatures than the pariah is usually made to appear on canvas, and as he exists in his feral state. They are certainly far removed from the mastiff or Mollossian type, which Virgil would lead us to believe the shepherds' dogs were; and, in the absence of sundry goats (not swine) in the background, these herdsmen's dogs of our modern artist, might be taken for wild animals being scared from the patriarch's flocks by the lovely vision of Minerva. But the same hand has treated us to some even more collie-like dogs than the above, in his two paintings, "The Wounded Adonis" and "Adonis' Farewell."

It would be interesting to know where the great artist obtained his suggestion as to the colour he gives these dogs, five of them in the second picture accompanying the hero on a hunting excursion.

Hunting he loved, but love he laughed to scorn.

These animals, fawning upon and leaping around their master, possess heads of the same type and with the same kindly, sagacious expression in their features as seen in our best shepherds' dogs of to-day. In colour they are varying shades of so-called sable, fawn and orange, and black and tan, the fashionable hue to be seen on the show bench, as rich and bright as the handsomest to be found at the late Crystal Palace and Birmingham exhibitions, and with the white collar round their neck and white breasts likewise. One generally believed these collies, rich orange sable in colour, were of modern manufacture, bred to attract the eye and please the taste of their owner and of the judge in the ring. Riviere on canvas tells us a different story, and makes us afraid to consider these two lovely works mythologically quite correct. Well enough they will please the student of the dog who wishes to make that of the shepherd the ideal from which all other varieties have sprung, and it is right perhaps that so handsome a huntsman should be accompanied by equally handsome dogs. Still, as a pack they do not seem likely animals to cope successfully with the

> Foul, grim, and urchin-snouted boar.

that killed Adonis, from whose blood the fair anemone was said to spring.

In some quarters astonishment is at times expressed that in the Old and New Testaments, in which so much is written of flocks and shepherds, so little is said as to dogs used for the protection of the former. As a fact no allusion whatever is made in the New Testament to shepherds' dogs of any kind, and, in the Old Testament, only in Job does the diligent searcher after knowledge find any verse which gives the inference that at the time the book was written dogs of some kind were used as assistants to those who looked after the flocks. The passage in question is to be found in chapter 30, verse 1, and is as follows: "Whose fathers I would have disdained to have set with the dogs of my flocks."

This, then, is the only allusion throughout the whole of the Scriptures which can be taken to mean the sheep dog. The Jews considered the dog an unclean beast, as they are said to have done all quadrupeds that had cloven hoofs or did not chew the cud. Such being the case there is little wonder that so useful an animal as the shepherds' dog should fail to meet with his deserts from Jewish historians.

Dr. Tristram, in his Natural History of the Bible, is very meagre in the information he gives about the dog. His illustration of the Syrian dog is in some respects by no means unlike the modern collie, although more wolf-like in general character, especially in the shape of his body. He says that the Jews, not being a hunting people, did not utilise the instinct of the dog for the pursuit of game. On the contrary the Egyptians had several varieties of the dog trained for domestic purposes—some for hunting, others as pets, holding them in peculiar estimation. "They saw in the horizon," says M. Blaze in his History of the Dog (Paris, 1843), "a superb star, which appeared always at the precise time when the over-flowing of the Nile commenced, and they gave to it the name of Sirius. This Sirius is a god; the dog renders us a service; it is a god," said they. "The dog thus came to be regarded as the god of the river, which the people represented with the body of a man and the head of a dog. This river god was also given a genealogy, bearing the name of Anubis, son of Osiris; its image was placed at the entrance of the temple of Isis and Osiris, and subsequently at the gates of all the temples in Egypt." (The latter possibly was in honour of Osiris, who has the credit of being the introducer of civilisation into Egypt.) Blaze proceeds to say, "The dog being the symbol of vigilance, it was thus intended to warn princes of their constant duty to watch over the welfare of their people. The dog was worshipped principally at Hermopolis the Great, and ultimately in all towns in Egypt. Juvenal writes: 'Whole cities worship the dog; not one Diana.' At a subsequent period Cynopolis, the 'City of the Dog' was built in the dog's honour, and there the priests celebrated its festivals in great splendour."

Other writers say that Anubis was represented as bearing a dog's head, because, when Osiris proceeded upon his Indian expedition, Anubis accompanied him clothed in dog skins. This is, however, a doubtful statement, as some assert that Anubis was clad in the skin of a sheep, and not in that of a dog. Whichever of the two stories be correct, there is no doubt the dog that guarded the property and the flocks of the Egyptians was thoroughly honoured, his popularity travelled rapidly westward, and the worship of the dog god came to be intermingled with the religious ceremonies of other nations. Lucan says, "We have received into our Roman temples thine Isis, and divinities half dog." . . . The fire-worshippers of Persia paid divine honour to the dog, and he is still held in deep veneration by the Parsees.

In allusion to the quotation from Job already given, Canon Tristram says the dogs were only used as guards, to protect the herds and flocks from wolves and jackals, and not to drive them. When dogs were first instructed in the art of driving sheep, and the ordinary purposes for which a well-trained collie is required at the present day, there is nothing to show.

That they were not so utilised in Great Britain to any great extent three or four hundred years ago I take to be a fact, because throughout the whole of Shakespere's plays not a single allusion is made to the shepherd's dog. The ordinary dog of course appears often enough, and so does the shepherd, but any combination of the two is not to be met with. Had shepherds' dogs been in common use when the great dramatist and poet lived, some reference or other would doubtless have been made to them, and, although I cannot believe that the English farmstead in the sixteenth century was without its dogs for some other purpose than sporting, the conclusion must naturally be reached that they were certainly not so much used in connection with the sheep and cattle as is the case to-day.

The learned Ulysses Aldrovandus, who wrote a gigantic work in Latin on Natural History, died in 1607, and some part of his *magnum opus* was published after his death. His allusions to the "villaticus canis," the farm dog, are particularly interesting and valuable, for his critics said "All his writings are marked by fulness of knowledge and the most reverent spirit." Dr. Caius (1550) gives *Canis villaticus* as the ban-dog, which he describes as a mastiff, "terrible and frightful to behold, and more fierce and fell than any Arcadian curre . . . They are serviceable against the foxe and badger, to drive wild and tame swyne out of medowes, pastures, glebe landes, and places planted with fruite, to bayte and take the bull by the eare when occasion so requireth." A good all-round dog; and if not useful in this country at the time the learned doctor wrote, *Canis villaticus* had been used for similar purposes centuries before, a watch dog rather than the dog of the shepherd. Of the latter Aldrovandus says, "In build he resembles the hound; he ought to be gentle to his own household, savage to those outside it, and not to be taken in by caresses. He should be robust, with a muscular body, and noisy in his deep bark, so that by his bold baying, he may threaten on all sides and frighten away prowlers. He should have a fierce light in his eyes, portending the lightning attack by his teeth on the rash enemy. He should be black in his coat in order to appear more fearful to thieves in the day-light, and being of the same shade as night itself—to be able to make his way quite unseen by enemies and thieves."

Aldrovandus next proceeds to tell us how to make a

white dog black, a piece of dishonest practice which of late years has been in vogue to a certain extent, especially so far as darkening what might be the white breast of a black and tan terrier. One was hardly prepared to find that any persons would have found it to their advantage to act so dishonestly with a dog hundreds of years ago, when the ordinary reader would little imagine "faking" was in vogue. However, here is the author's mode of procedure: "The country dog may, however, happen to be white, although in other respects he may be very good. The first thing to do then is to make him of a black colour. Take some quick-lime and let it effervesce in water along with a lump of litharge, and if you rub the dog with this it will easily blacken him." Rather a drastic recipe, and one which must have been used with great care. Our author notwithstanding, I believe the white dog uncoloured would do his duty quite as well, and be found of equal use with the black one, be the latter artificially made so or in his natural habit.

These same dogs that Aldrovandus describes, according to Bellonius, "in Turkey have no individual owners, consequently do not go inside the houses, merely having a shelter stuck up for them in the yard under which they sleep; and alongside the walls of the house there are certain stone troughs into which bread, scraps, and bones are thrown, and on these they feed. They protect the place where they are brought up, and from it they drive away prowling dogs and wolves."

Blondus says shepherds could not defend a large flock of sheep from prowling wolves without their sheep dogs that are armed with iron collars like that faithful shepherd's dog referred to by the poet—"safeguard of his property, which lies all night on the doorstep." In the old days, amongst the Romans, wolves increased to such an extent that owners of sheep were obliged to keep a pack of fifty dogs to guard the flocks. Conradus Heresbach selected males to perform these duties in preference to females, although, the same writer says, "splayed bitches are equally as watchful and most ready with their teeth." Heresbach, contrary to Aldrovandus, preferred white as the desirable colour for a sheep dog, in order that he might better be distinguished from a distance by wolves and thieves, and avoided. Varro recommends a sheep dog of large size, and loud in his bark. Niphus, like Virgil, calls the sheep dog "mastivus," and the shepherds' dogs of Epirus were celebrated for their excellence.

Aldrovandus proceeds to say that as dogs of this class have to spend most of their lives along with flocks and herds, they are to be entirely fed on whey. Sometimes they are given barley meal cooked in milk and water, and occasionally beans are mixed therewith. Columella, another ancient authority on the matter of sheep dogs, forbids them touching the flesh of the animals they look after in order that they may not become savage towards them; and a third writer, at a little later period, says it is "very difficult to call in sheep dogs that have once acquired a taste for raw meat."

Although some of these notes from Aldrovandus do not bear very closely upon my subject, others do, and collectively they prove that the shepherd's dog of his day and preceding it, was more or less a powerful, savage animal, to be feared by marauders either biped or quadruped. Not a word is said as to his sagacity in driving his flocks or herds, or collecting the stragglers which fresh sweet pasture may have tempted to wander away from the main body. The sheep dog of that era bore a greater resemblance to the modern Pyrenean guard dog than it did to the collie of the British Isles as it is known now, and fifty such powerful animals must have proved a formidable pack for the farmer to feed and the shepherds to look after.

As to feeding these dogs on whey (which Virgil also alludes to in a quotation made earlier in this chapter), barley meal, &c., in order to prevent them acquiring a taste for meat, some of our modern agriculturists might take a lesson. Most of the lamb and sheep worrying that takes place periodically is done by the farmers' own dogs, that have possibly acquired a "taste for mutton" through being allowed to feed upon a dead lamb or sheep which the shepherd has been too lazy or indolent to bury. Or when they have done the latter, possibly so little earth has been placed over the carcases that passing dogs are not prevented smelling them, which, as opportunity affords, scratch up the decomposing filth, filling themselves to repletion thereon. Many good dogs have thus been utterly ruined by the carelessness of their owners; and when a sheep dog or collie once gets this liking for "mutton," he waits not his turn for a dead sheep, but, prowling out at night time, kills one for himself. Possibly, he carefully covers over the remains of the carcase, to which he will return the following day and continue so to do until the bones are picked, and scraps of wool, blown about by the breeze, remain the only signs of the tragedy which has been enacted. This is a subject which will be returned to later on.

Dr. Caius, or Keyes, in his "Treatise on Englishe Dogges," already alluded to, and the earliest work on the subject in the English language when it came to be translated from the Latin by Abraham Fleming, includes the shepherd's dog in the fourth section of his dissertation. He alludes to them as "dogs of a coarse kind serving for many necessary uses, called in Latin *Canis pastoralis*." Any illustration of this dog, as he appeared in the sixteenth century, would no doubt have been most interesting, and in the absence of such drawing, readers must trust to their imagination to supply the deficiency.

The quaintness of the writer and his more or less interesting description must be my excuse for quoting a great portion of the chapter on the "shepherd's hound," which he says "is very necessary and profitable for the avoiding of harms and inconveniences which may come to men by means of beasts. Our shepherd's dog is not huge and vast, and big, but of an indifferent stature and growth, because it has not to deal with the bloodthirsty wolf, since there be none in England, which happy and fortunate benefit is to be ascribed to the puissant Prince Edgar, who to the intent the whole country might be evacuated and quite cleared from wolves, charged and commanded the Welshmen (who were pestered with these butcherly beasts above measure) to pay him yearly tribute which was (note the wisdom of the king) three hundred wolves. Some there be which write that Ludwall Prince of Wales paid yearly to King Edgar three hundred wolves in the name of an exaction (as we have said before), and that by the means hereof, within the compass and term of four years, none of those noisome and pestilent beasts were left on the coasts of England and Wales. This Edgar wore the crown royal and bare the sceptre imperial of this kingdom about the year of our Lord 959. Since which time we read that no wolf has been seen in England, bred within the bounds and borders of this country, although there have been divers brought over from beyond the seas for greediness of gain and to make money for gazing and gaping, staring and standing to see them, being a strange beast, rare and seldom seen in England. But to return to our shepherd's dog. This dog, either at the hearing of his master's voice or at the wagging of his fist, or at his shrill and hoarse whistling and hissing, bringeth the wandering wethers and straying sheep into the self-same place where his master's will and work is to have them, whereby the shepherd reapeth the benefit, namely, that with little labour and no toil of moving his feet he may rule and guide his flock according to his own desire, either to have them go forward or stand still, or to draw backward, or to turn this way or to take that way. For it is not in England as it is in France, as it is in Flanders, as it is in Syria, as it is in Tartary, where the sheep follow the shepherd, for here in our country the shepherd followeth the sheep. And sometimes the straying sheep, when no dog runneth before them, nor goeth about and beside them, gather themselves into a flock when they hear the shepherd whistle, for fear of the dog (as I imagine), remembering this (if unreasoning creatures may be reported to have memory) that the dog commonly runneth out at his master's warrant, which is his whistle. This have we oftentimes marked when taking our journey from town to town; when we have heard a shepherd whistle, we have reined in our horse and stood still a pace to see the proof and trial of this matter. Furthermore, with this dog doth the shepherd take the sheep to slaughter, and to be healed if they be sick, and no hurt or harm is done by the dogs to the simple creature."

I have endeavoured to somewhat modernize the quaint spelling, and caused one or two alterations in other particulars, in order to make this oldest record we have of the working of shepherd's dog more intelligible to the reader than it appears in the reprint from which the extract is copied.

In the volumes of the Royal Zoological Society there is an engraving of the Hare Indian Dog, evidently the same animal which Youatt illustrates. This is a handsome creature, somewhat resembling a collie in expression, but longer in the head, and with legs and body built more on the lines of an unusually heavily made Eastern greyhound. The Arctic explorer, Dr. Richardson, discovered this dog on the Mackenzie river, and describes it as somewhat like a Pomeranian in appearance, with broad, erect ears, sharp at the tips; the tail pendant, with a slight curl upwards near the tip. The feet of the Hare Indian dog are thickly clothed with fur, enabling him to run upon the snow with rapidity and ease. It is a dog nearer allied in appearance to our modern collie than any other of the varieties used as guard dogs or beasts of burden in semi-civilized countries.

The Samoyede sledge dogs—a class for which was made at the Kennel Club's show in February, 1889—are white in colour, much resembling a modern collie crossed with a Pomeranian in appearance. They are smaller dogs than those used in the Arctic regions in drawing sledges, although their importer, Mr. F. L. James, said they are ordinarily trained for that purpose.

Here are a number of animals evidently of varying types and sizes, all used, as it were, for domestic purposes, many of them valuable as guards to the flocks and herds; others acting the part of horses as beasts of burden; all more or less domesticated. Did they spring from the same stock? At this juncture all information appears to come to an end, and the origin of the dog, the shepherd's dog in particular, is as far off being found as ever.

Although Darwin considers the dog to be descended from several wild species, he cannot believe that animals closely resembling the Italian greyhound, the bloodhound, the bulldog, pug dog, Blenheim spaniel, &c., so unlike all wild *canidæ*, ever existed in a state of nature. In their production the great scientist says, "there has been an immense amount of inherited variation," but he is not very explicit as to the manner in which this was brought about. Personally, I see little difficulty in producing a variety given proper crosses, and say fifteen or twenty years time in which to work. Darwin thinks the possibility of making distinct races by crossing has been greatly exaggerated.

During the past quarter of a century extraordinary progress has been made in the matter of breeding to type in dogs and in other animals. The various toy spaniels, including the King Charles and the Blenheims, are very different in appearance, and especially in the shape of their heads and their faces, from what they were a generation past. The bulldogs the same, and to a smaller degree the change is noted in other varieties. This appears to have been brought about gradually, and in the first instance, accidentally almost and without any particular object in view. Later the exhibition of dogs caused even greater variation. Owners by mere chance in breeding have had produced to them a dog with one particular point enormously exaggerated; this has proved attractive, so the breeder has continued to, as it were, manufacture by judicious crossing other exaggerated properties, which have come to the neglect of other, possibly equally important, points. So the changes are brought about.

With the exception of the shepherd's dog, deerhound, foxhound, and greyhound, there is not one strain of British dog at the present time which bears much more than a great resemblance to his variety as it was known a hundred years ago. If such changes as these can be made in a comparatively short time, in the first instance, brought about, as I have said, almost accidentally, one may take for granted that thousands of years can have produced proportionate variations. Varieties have grown and are still increasing. Germany has of late given us the Leonberg dog; America the Chesapeke Bay dog; Britain, not to be behind, has produced the Paisley terrier; the Airedale terrier, too, is a comparatively new variety, and one that produces its puppies true to type and thoroughly distinct in appearance from any of our other terriers. A hundred years hence more changes in our dogs will have been wrought, and may-be the so-called fancy varieties will come to be " improved " until past recognition.

In an earlier volume, "The Fox Terrier," published by Horace Cox, 346, Strand, I showed, I fancy, pretty plainly that this fashionable little dog, now white in colour, with black and brown, or tan, or yellow markings, was originally a pure black and tan in hue, this change having so far been produced accidentally. Take our modern sheep dog, the collie in fact, and examine him carefully, he will not be found very far removed in expression from some of the semi-wild dogs still known. The dingo for instance, the ordinary Esquimaux, and some of the handsome domesticated Chinese dogs, so-called Chow-Chows, which they are not, bear a very striking resemblance in head and countenance to the modern sheep dog. That the collie is nearly allied to all these I do not doubt for a moment.

In Scotland there are those who believe the hard-haired Scotch terrier, the deerhound, and the collie, are one and the same dog. Though the bodies and general forms of the three are very diverse, their heads in shape and expression much resemble each other. Their ears are much the same in carriage and character, and the dispositions of the three varieties are similar or would be so were they all brought up and reared under the same system. The coats or jackets of the deerhound and terrier are both hard and crisp, and much the same in colour, fawns or light browns being occasionally found in each, the prevailing shades being various degrees of brown or dark brindle. The collie, on the other hand, has a longer coat of a different colour, perhaps the result of crossing for fancy rather than for useful purposes. No one who possesses any eye for a dog, can fail to notice some resemblance between these three native dogs so unlike in some particulars, so similar in others.

Much has at times been said about crossing the sheepdog with the black and tan or Gordon setter; the latter was most probably crossed with the sheep dog. The Scottish deerhound is a much more likely cross, and some years ago I struck a trail, which, I thought, if followed to the end, would result in making a discovery of some deerhound strain in our modern sheepdog. Although I failed to follow out the line, personally I believe that the variety of dog to which this volume is dedicated at a not very remote period received a considerable impression of this cross. Some twenty years ago Mr. John Rigg, of the Windermere Hotel, in the lake district of the north of England, exhibited a very handsome dog called Rap, and with him took several prizes at the north country shows in those days. Now Rap, though a thorough sheepdog in expression and form, in his fawn colour, shape of head, ears, and texture of coat showed a most remarkable resemblance to a deerhound. About the same time and earlier dogs somewhat resembling this one were occasionally met with in the north, and they most certainly contained the cross I suggest. It appears to have died out now, or become amalgamated to such an extent as to be imperceptible in the modern productions. I wrote inquiring from Mr. Rigg as to the pedigree of his favourite, and alas! it had none. It was purchased by its owner from a cattle dealer at Kendal fair, from whence it was taken to its new quarters eight miles away by rail. Next day Rap was missing, and was found to have gone home to Bentham in Yorkshire, some thirty miles distance, at the earliest opportunity. The road was unknown to the dog, but on being taken back to Windermere, and being kindly treated there, he never repeated the journey.

As I said the pedigree could not be traced, Rap looked half deerhound, and Mr. Rigg himself said he always thought his favourite contained some "staghound" (deerhound) blood. The sagacity of this dog could not be surpassed, his late owner has been on the look-out for his equal ever since; and need I say the search has been unsuccessful. In case any of our modern admirers of the collie be desirous of obtaining a distinct cross, I would suggest the trial of deerhound blood in preference to that of the setter. With the former they would, at any rate, not lose that "long, lean head" so much fancied by a section of breeders. Possibly an improved coat could be obtained, and the intelligence of the animal would not be likely to deteriorate.

So much for the origin of the sheep dog, as he is known in his British varieties; the Scotch collie, the smooth-coated sheep dog, and the old English bob-tailed sheep dog. Other so-called varieties are but local names for the same articles.

## CHAPTER II.

THE COLLIE—THE MEANING OF THE WORD—THE
"SPORTSMAN'S CABINET"—TAIL CUTTING—NORTH
COUNTRY COLLIES—IN LITERATURE AND ART—HIS
CHARACTER—WORK v. SHOW.

OF late years the handsome and intelligent collie has, with the equally good-looking and engaging fox terrier, divided the fashionable world in its love for the dog. Both, in their way, are perfect as companions, but the shorter coat of the terrier, his smaller size, and better adaptability for the house, have given him priority, and as a fashionable companion the collie has had to play second fiddle. Long before he came to be an inhabitant of the drawing-room Mrs. Rawdon Crawley (*née* Becky Sharp) asked her dear Captain to obtain a shepherd's dog for her; not a dog in fact, but a companion, who would protect our heroine from the scandals of the gossips, and allow her to go about with a legitimate protector. Thackeray little knew when he wrote his best of novels, that the shepherd's dog was in the end to become the ladies' companion he had suggested, and as it now appears in the form of the Scotch collie.

But what is a collie? ask my readers, and why the name, and why not the older one of shepherd's dog? The derivation of this same word has excited the curiosity of many writers, leading them into the troubles of research with about as much result as has been reached as to the origin of the dog itself. Until within recent years the word collie was used in conjunction with the word dog, thus your friend owned a collie dog or a Scotch collie dog, as the case might be. A collie dog was just a dog used in connection with a "collie," a variety of sheep common to Scotland, and which the Dictionary of Husbandry, published in 1743, spelling it colley, describes as "such sheep as have black faces and legs. The wool of these sheep is very harsh with hairs, and not so white as other sheep." Shakespere uses the word collie in one or two places, with a similar meaning of blackened or darkened, thus in the first scene of the first act of "A Midsummer Night's Dream," Lysander speaks to Hermia thus :

> Brief as the lightning in the collied night.

and in " Othello " the passage occurs :

> Having my best judgment collied.

Blackened or darkened the word, now quite obsolete, means; derived from the Anglo-Saxon "col," black; and so the black-faced and black-legged sheep came to be called "colleys," and the dogs that drove them colley dogs. In due course the word dog was dropped, and as the name of this Scotch sheep was discontinued, so far as they were concerned it became usurped by a variety of the canine race, and what was once a sheep, by this odd process of transformation became a dog. So, in fact, only by custom and privilege is the collie a dog. The former, too, might be something else altogether, for in Ireland the loach, a small bearded fish, which lives mostly under the stones, a capital bait for salmon, is known as the "colley," and always talked of as such. Again, in hawking, a hawk is said "to colly" when she stretches out her neck straight forward; and there is the same word in a different meaning, as "to colly" to embrace round the neck. Still this word in its commonest use means to darken or blacken. A friend of mine says that about sixty years ago in Northamptonshire there lived a man who bore the nickname of "Colly," a *nom de plume* arising from his peculiarly dark complexion and his coal-black hair. Thus it will be seen that our dog has in this case obtained more than his just rights, and the poor black-faced Scotch sheep with its "coarse wool-like hairs" is robbed of its somewhat euphonious, if comparatively obsolete name.

Hugh Dalziel, in his monograph on the breed, alludes to the passage in Chaucer, where "Coll, our dog" occurs, and believes it may be in reference to the colour of the animal. There is no reason to suppose that "Coll" was anything but the name of the dog, as "Jack" or "Gyp" might have been. Nor is it at all likely that the word was derived from the "col," already alluded to, as "embracing round the neck," because in many cases modern collies have had and still have a stretch of broad white hairs round their necks—white collars, in fact. St. Bernards have these white collars much more pronounced, and in this large variety of the dog a specimen is not considered perfect without such a distinguishing mark with a white blaze down the face.

I think I have produced sufficient evidence to prove how the word collie, as applied to the shepherd's dog, came to be obtained, and, so far as can be made out, Thomas Bewick, the eminent wood engraver, was the earliest writer who used the word as applied to the dog. The first edition of his Natural History was printed in 1790. It contains a portrait of "The coaly," another form in which the word is to be found, and the great master in wood engraving was fond of transferring his ideal sheepdog to the charming little tail-pieces which adorn so many works. Bewick's collie was evidently a dark-coloured, probably a black and white, dog, with the white collar around his neck, the white frill on his breast, sometimes two white forelegs, and generally with semi-erect ears. There was no mistaking Bewick's collies, he drew them full of character, just as they were found, unadulterated and unimproved, round about Newcastle and on the borders, where they earned their living by looking after the sheep, and not by taking long railway journeys from town to town to bring grist into the coffers of their owners—the modern duties of all good-looking dogs.

The Rev. W. Bingley, M.A., in his memoir of "British Quadrupeds" (1809), publishes one of Howitt's lovely etchings, which is called the "shepherd's dog," and not the English sheepdog, the expression other contemporary writers most frequently used. Here we have a black and white dog driving, at a rapid pace, a small flock of sheep on the mountains or fells. His head is long, ears semi-erect, and he possesses a long bushy tail, which, judging from its position, would, when its owner was walking, be carried gracefully drooping with the end just turned upwards—

A gawkie tail, wi' upward curl.

The form of the dog in Howitt's etching is excellent;

there is a fair quantity of coat, a broad white collar, the blaze down the face; and had this shepherd's dog been given a milder and more intelligent expression of countenance, his form appears quite good enough to have taken a prize at modern shows had he lived to-day.

Unfortunately, the painstaking Bingley is woefully meagre in his letter-press description, and all he does is to give the shepherd's dog a character for instinct and sagacity "superior to all others, for, whilst the rest require great care and attention to train them to labour, this animal applies himself, without any difficulty, to that which he is usually appropriated. His usefulness alone has been the recommendation to preserve the species, since no dog can go through a more extensive variety of duty, nor does anyone perform more services to his master than this."

This is not altogether complimentary to the handsomeness of our friend, whose actual beauty at the present day places him on quite a fashionable basis, and makes him one of our most popular varieties of the dog. Nor is Bingley quite correct as to a shepherd's dog requiring no training. Some strains there are that do require less than others, but both training and continued work are required to make even the most sagacious of his race perform his difficult duties in a proper fashion. Had working trials for sheep-dogs been in practice when the "Memoir of British Quadrupeds" was compiled, its reverend and respected author would not have written as he has done. He does not allude in any case to the shepherd's dog as the collie, so here again we have proof that, excepting, perhaps, locally in parts of Scotland and in the extreme north of England, where Thomas Bewick dwelt, the shepherd's dog was not known by such a name at that time.

## Reinagle's Sheep Dog.        25

One would not expect to find much information on this subject in the "Sportsman's Cabinet," two handsome volumes admirably illustrated, by P. Reinagle, R.A., published in 1803 at seven guineas, and now worth considerably more than that sum. Still, several pages are devoted to a description of the shepherd's dog, and John Scott engraves from one of Reinagle's pictures a portrait of that animal. This is an old-fashioned semi-bobtailed sheep dog, grey or blue and white in colour, strong in limbs, long and broad in ears, and with a hard wiry-looking coat. Not a bad dog of the stamp of the old-fashioned drover's dog still seen, but unpleasantly light yellow eyes produce a ferocious and treacherous expression which would be quite wrong at any time in an animal of this variety. This dog, although usually used for driving cattle, is here on the hills—Welsh hills, probably—looking after a flock of sheep, more like Southdowns than anything else. They are certainly neither the small black-faced Welsh or Scotch sheep, nor the Herdwicks of the north of England. But artists will at times take liberties with their subjects, often enough, as in this instance, to the extent of quite spoiling the truthfulness of what otherwise would have been a pleasant engraving.

The writer of the article is most eulogistic in his praises of the dog which he calls "a peculiar breed," now known as the sheepdog in every rural district of the kingdom. It is the "most timid, obedient, placid, serene, and grateful in creation; he seems studiously conscious of the purposes for which he was formed, and is never so perceptibly gratified as when affording the most incessant proofs of his unsullied integrity. Instinctively prone to industry, he is alive to the slightest sensation of his employer, and would rather double and treble the watch-line of circumspection than be seen indulging in a state of neglectful indolence. The breed is propagated and preserved with the greatest respect to purity in the northern parts of Yorkshire, as well as in the Highlands of Scotland, where, in the extensive tracts and uncultivated wilds, their services exceed description."

The writer proceeds in similarly eulogistic and ponderous strains, which, no doubt, are all very well in their way, but one would very much have preferred some few lines descriptive of the dog, of his coat, size, colour and general character, in place of the adulatory comments and anecdotic string of stories which follow. Proceeding, however, with some few lines more of the "Sportsman's Cabinet" story, the writer continues: "Constitutionally calm, patient, and philosophic, the sheep dog appears totally lost to every appearance of novelty, and insensible to every attraction beyond the protection and indefatigable preservation of the flock committed to his charge. In the most sequestered and remote spots, dreary wilds, and lofty mountains, almost inaccessible to man, the dog becomes an incredible and trusty substitute; for, once initiated into the groundwork of his office, he soon acquires a perfect knowledge of the extent of his walk, as well as of every individual of his flock; and will as regularly select his own, and disperse obtruders as the most faithful and attentive shepherd in existence. This becomes the more extraordinary to the contemplative mind, when it is recollected what immense flocks are seen to cover the downy hills of Hants and Wilts, as far as the eye can reach without control; and to know that by a single signal from the shepherd this faithful, sagacious animal, replete with energy, vigilance, and activity, will make his circle so as to surround a flock of hundreds and bring them within any compass that may be required.

"The sheep dog is so completely absorbed in what seems the sole business and employment of his life, that he does not bestow a look, or indulge a wish beyond the constant protection of the trust reposed in him, and to execute the commands of his master, which he is always incessantly anxious to receive, and in fact is invariably looking for by every solicitous attention it is possible to conceive. Inured to all weathers, fatigue, and hunger, he is the least voracious of his species, subsists upon little, and may be considered truly emblematical of content. Though there is an appearance of somniferous indolence in the exterior, it is by no means a constitutional mark of habitual inability; on the contrary, the sagacity, fidelity, and comprehensive penetrations of this kind of dog is equal to any other, but that there is a thoughtful or expressive gravity annexed to this particular race, as if they were absolutely conscious of their own utility in business of importance, and the value of the stock so confidently committed to their care."

No doubt a really good collie, well trained and accustomed to his work, is the most sensible quadruped in creation, the huge elephant alone excepted. But the reader must not get into his mind that all collies are equally good alike; as in other races of dogs, there are both good, bad, and indifferent. The continual association of the shepherd's dogs with their owners have given them their unusual degree of intelligence: they live in the house with him, they accompany him on his daily rounds to look after the flocks or the herds, they feed with their master as a rule, and are looked on by him as a part and parcel of his farm stock. They were thus a hundred years ago and more, they remain so now, though their popularity with the masses and the procedure of dog show business has certainly not improved the collie from an intellectual point of view. The exhibitions have improved his coat in profuseness, have caused the head to lengthen abnormally, and produced him prettier in colour and handsomer in his markings. He is more pampered and petted than he used to be, but to a great extent any advancement in his really legitimate calling has been sadly neglected. For here again we find that a dog, to be in good, hard, working condition, is not in that form of long, flossy coat likely to prove attractive to the judge in the show ring. And in the latter position his progress has within the most recent two decades been extraordinary.

From the beginning of the present century to past its middle appears a long gap, but, during that period little appears to have been heard of the collie dog outside the farm on which he was employed. He was found useful, and kept for the purpose of attending to the cattle and sheep, as the case might be.

Allusion might be made here to the custom that once prevailed of cutting the tails of farmers' dogs, in order, either that they could be better distinguished from those kept for sporting purposes by the man whose social position and wealth allowed him to do so, or to prevent them becoming adepts at coursing hares, foxes, and rabbits; as the removal of the caudal appendage prevented the creature from turning so well when running as he would do were he in his natural condition. When the dog taxes were first introduced in 1796 the custom was almost entirely abolished, although here and there it died a somewhat lingering death. With it expired the last of the relics of the feudal times and the old Forest Laws, when the villain was compelled to amputate the toes of his house or shepherd's dog in order that it could not destroy the game of his lord and master, to whom he was little better than a serf. I think there is no doubt that the custom of docking the dog was a modification of this most barbarous and painful custom both performed with similar ends in view.

Indeed, that this was so must be taken for granted, and the expression a "curtail" dog was by no means uncommon three hundred years ago, or even more recently. The word in this sense is still to be found in some of the older and more complete dictionaries. Todd, in his excellent edition of Johnson, says the word "curtail," as applied to the dog, means "a dog lawed or mutilated according to the Forest Laws, whose tail is cut off, and is therefore hindered in coursing," and Avon's immortal bard in his "Comedy of Errors" makes Dromio of Syracuse say, "I, amazed, ran from her as a witch; and I think if my breast had not been made of faith and my heart of steel, she had transformed me to a *curtail dog*, and made me turn i' the wheel." A similar word is put into the mouth of Pistol, in Act II., Scene I., of the "Merry Wives of Windsor," when he says, "Hope is a curtall dog in some affairs."

Thus have we the origin of the word "cur" as yet applied to the shepherd's dog in many parts of the country; still owing to its unpleasant associations and dual meaning, the word will no doubt become obsolete in the course of a few generations.

The custom of docking dogs had, however, prevailed so long that I am firmly of opinion that from it arose the strain of tailless sheepdogs, which are still to be met with and are by no means uncommon. Some varieties are less frequently found than others, but I have observed smooth bob-tailed dogs, the ordinary rough-coated ones likewise, as well as the commoner drover's dogs, all born without tails or with the merest apology for the same. I am aware that there are opinions diverse to these of mine, but, although there has not yet been produced in this country a true variety of terrier which comes into the world with tails already shortened, occasional cases do occur. Two or three at least have come under my own personal knowledge, and, so long ago as eighteen years, I myself bred two fox terriers of prize strains born with their tails already shortened. They were not good specimens, so came to be drowned; but no doubt from a dog so born, mated with a bitch bearing a similar peculiarity, a race of bob-tailed fox terriers could in due course have been produced. As a fact, even in the pure strains of the old English sheep dog, which are supposed to be whelped without a tail at all, caudal appendages varying in length are even oftener produced than not.

Bearing on the same subject come the Schipperkes from the Dutch canal boats, black little dogs recently introduced into this country, and usually born without tails. Surely, nature in the first instance never made them so, and continued docking as a process of undesirable civilisation, must have produced the result. Both in this variety and in the natural bob-tailed Old English sheepdogs, puppies with and without tails are produced in the same litters. We search in vain for an instance where nature has produced tailless specimens of the *canidæ* or even of the *carnivoræ* in their feral state, the nearest approach thereto being in the lynxes, a race thoroughly distinct as compared with any of the species from which the common dog may have sprung.

These facts, taken into consideration with reasons already given, lead me to come to the conclusion already expressed, that all tailless dogs are more or less artificial productions, the results of some of the anomalies of our boasted civilisation. Arguments against my supposition may be produced in the case of terriers with their ears cut, and hounds with their aural appendages rounded, but neither is an exactly analogous case, and the effect on the system, through the spine and muscles, is much more likely to be of a permanent character where the tail is operated upon than where the infliction is confined to the ears.

Following the discontinuance of the custom of cutting farmers' dogs' tails and other changes, sheepdogs had to pay the same impost to the Legislature as other varieties of the canine race. This arrangement was, however, not sufficiently satisfactory as to be permanent, for in 1878, when the dog regulations were again revised, special individual exemptions for dogs used in farm work had to be obtained from the excise, a method of arrangement which remains in operation at the present time. Bearing this in mind, agriculturists cannot be too careful in keeping such exempted dogs solely to their natural work, for in case they allow them to assist in a day's rabbit catching on the farm, the licence is required, and the farmer lays himself open to a prosecution for keeping such a dog without paying the usual seven shillings and sixpence for the good of his country.

The popularity of the collie made much greater progress in some counties and localities than in others, for, where sheep formed the staple commodity of the farm, he was found to be an absolute necessity. This was especially the case in the more mountainous districts, such as are found in Wales, in the North of England, and in Scotland, where each farm, according to the size of the flock kept, had dogs in proportion. As a rule, on the smaller holdings, when such were not at work, they accompanied their owner to the market or wherever he went, even to the extent of following him to church on a Sunday. The story is told that a stranger visiting a portion of the Cumberland lake district, asked a shepherd he met on the fells what kind of a congregation they had at the little chapel down below on the Sunday? "Why," replied the native, "t' parson's a rare good sort, an' last Sunday, when I went past, thar war ten sheepdogs liggin' int' porch and t' churchyard." The shepherd so judging the size of the congregation, and leaving his questioner to infer likewise. Odd men were some of these shepherd dalesmen, writing of forty or fifty years ago —mostly the farmers themselves or the farmers' sons. They are not yet honoured or distinguished by being placed on canvas as ideals of manly beauty and figure, with their plaids gracefully thrown round them and sitting on a heather-clad bank, playing upon some impossible looking instrument, with their dog gazing up in surprise. Still, the Cumberland and Westmoreland shepherd is in many cases a character, and by no means without his share of retort when anything of the kind is required.

One there was who had given his parson cause to complain of his neglect in attending church on a Sunday. On a certain occasion, when morning service had been concluded, the minister met his parishioner returning from the fells with his dog at his heels, and judged this a proper time to administer a little fatherly advice as to the neglect of religious observances. "Good day, John," said the parson. "Good day to you, sir," said the farmer. "And," continued the parson, "I see, John, you have been looking after your flock, as I have been looking after mine!" "Aye, aye, sir," came the retort; "I hope, parson, as you found none o' your flock int' wicks, as I found some of mine?" John rather rudely turning on his heels and walking away. But there was a great deal of pleasant familiarity between the dalesmen and their "priest," as he was called a few generations ago, and one is not quite sure whether the increased prudishness and pedantry of the times have been much to the religious improvement of such localities.

The continued association of the dog and the man was naturally likely to improve the sensibility of the former, and when the two, as it were, came to be seldom separated, the animal's rare instinct and sagacity were sure to be developed to an extraordinary extent. The shepherd has but to wave his hand in a certain direction, and away gallops his faithful friend to seek what is to be found, and the little flock is quickly gathered and brought right up to their master. One sheep may be missing. The dog goes back to seek it. The last one may be hurt and lame. The dog by its manner lets the shepherd know such is the case. "Bring in the cows," said a farmer friend of mine to his dog, which lay dozing at his feet, by the kitchen fire. Up jumps the fine old chap, and, darting through the door and the farmyard, is out across two or three fields, and, barking behind the kye, soon brings them to the shippon, where the farm-servants await to fodder them up for the night, or milk them, as the case may be. Such is the everyday work of the farm-dog, and he is almost always a collie now.

Away in the mountains of Scotland, on the fells of the North of England, and upon the hills of Wales the shepherd's dog becomes the most useful. There a couple of well-trained collies will do as much work as a dozen men; indeed, in many instances bipeds could not go through the task these hardly-wrought and carefully-trained quadrupeds pursue day after day. And they perform their labour so quietly, too; no hurry and bustle, no biting or barking, the sheep know they have met their master when they have a good dog to drive them.

Many writers have, from time to time, eulogised the sheep dog both in prose and poetry. Peter Pindar has in the latter touchingly related the love that existed between the old shepherd's dog and his old master, both grey with age, still "happy in love did they hobble along;" and when the poor dog lay down to rise no more, and dying licking Corin's hand, we are told—

> Not long after Tray did the shepherd remain,
> Who oft o'er his grave with true sorrow would bend;
> And when dying, thus feebly was heard the poor swain,
> "O bury me, neighbours, beside my poor friend."

Robert Burns, like almost all his countrymen, was much endeared to the collies of his native land, and in his "Twa Dogs," one of which came from the island where "sailors fish for cod;" the other Luath, one of his own fancy, has its character admirably described as follows:

> He was a gash and faithfu' tyke
> As ever lap a sleugh or dyke.
> His honest, sonsie, bausint face
> Aye gat him friends in ilka place.
> His breast was white, his towzie back
> Weel clad wi' coat o' glossy black.
> His gawkie tail, wi' upward curl,
> Hung ower his hurdies wi' a swurl.

Sir Walter Scott might have given us some of his verses in honour of the sheepdog, instead of doing so much to ennoble hounds of various kinds, and a peculiar strain of terrier which, without the great novelist's assistance, would probably not be known to-day, at any rate to the extent of its present popularity. Personally, I always regretted that the faithful, though cross-bred terrier, that accompanied young Gough during his fatal ascent of Helvellyn had not been a sheep dog. The latter would have made the more faithful companion, and might have been despatched for assistance when the unfortunate pedestrian became prostrate. These words to a well-trained collie, "Hie away home," and the dog would have gone, and by his manner let friends know that some accident had happened to his master. Melancholy as was the occurrence which formed the subject of one of Sir Walter's most sympathetic poems, it was rendered even more so by the supposition that the faithful terrier had prolonged his own life at the expense of his dead master's body, a horrible idea which with a collie could never have been suggested.

James Hogg (the Ettrick Shepherd), Professor Wilson, Tennyson, all appreciated this variety of dog to the utmost, but Wordsworth cared very little about dogs. His poems afforded every opportunity for him to do his share towards popularising the shepherd's dog, so common and faithful in his district of the lakes, but he allowed the idle boys to find the lost lamb

> Still swimming round and round.

In "The Evening Walk" Wordsworth, however, notices this dog a little more generously.

> Waving his hat, the shepherd, in the vale
> Directs his winding dog the cliffs to scale,—
> That barking, busy 'mid the glittering rocks
> Hunts, where he points, the intercepted flocks.

.Poor misanthropic Byron would possibly not have written in the vein he did had his dog been a collie.

> Perchance my dog will whine in vain,
>   Till fed by stranger hands;
> But long ere I come back again,
>   He'd tear me where he stands.

And how little shepherds' dogs were used, at any rate in the southern parts of our island, approaching a hundred years ago, may be inferred from the fact that no allusion is made to them in Robert Bloomfield's "The Farmer's Boy," possibly one of the pleasantest and most descriptive pastoral poems in our language.

With the artists of the present and of some previous generations, the shepherd's dog has been a great favourite. As already stated, Bewick was possibly the first to draw him correctly and picturesquely in the form as he is seen to-day, though Howitt, not very much later, followed the great wood engraver and his school in this respect. Landseer, who it may be said popularised the black and white Newfoundland, which now bears the name of the great painter, preferred the collie to all other varieties of dog, not excepting the Highland deerhound. The sympathetic expression of the shepherd's companion gave the artist an opportunity of transferring to canvas an effect which he could convey with his brush better than any other man. Herein lay Landseer's great skill, and if he at times (and Briton Riviere has followed him in this respect), gave to his dogs an expression too human, such has been a pleasing exaggeration, and one most satisfactory to the public. The collie was his favourite dog, and in one of his less known pictures, "The Connoisseurs," a portrait of the artist, the characters are supported by a sable and white typical collie, and a half-bred bloodhound. This picture is now in the possession of H.R.H. the Prince of Wales. "The Shepherd's Chief Mourner" again contains this dog as the principal object in one of the most popular pictures; and the same painter's "Collie Dogs," one a black and tan, the other a sable and white, likewise shows his fondness for this picturesque variety of the canine race. But Landseer painted many other pictures containing sheep dogs, and delineated them in a manner that has not been excelled since, and was never equalled before.

Year after year the exhibitions of the Royal Academy and of our other picture galleries prove the collie a favourite by the subjects hanging on their walls. On one occasion it may be seen in all rusticity by the dog endeavouring to get a stray lamb out of an unpleasant predicament ("Rescued," by Wallis Hunt, 1888); on another a more domestic subject is represented by a pretty little baby-boy crawling on all fours and looking up into the face of a handsome collie ("Can't you Talk?" by G. Holmes). The sheep dog in art is, however, a subject that might be dealt with almost in a volume by itself, and his bare mention in connection therewith is only required in a work of this description. Still, these pictures go to prove his popularity; possibly, some of the earlier ones have assisted his progress towards the high estimation in which he is now held by all classes, he being found equally at home in the cottage of the shepherd as in the palaces of our Royal Family. With Her Majesty the Queen the Scotch collie is a great favourite, and both at Balmoral and Windsor canine matters are almost entirely monopolised by several handsome specimens of the race, gentle, sensible creatures, always pleased to be caressed by hands more plebeian than are those of their Royal mistress.

The collie is admirably adapted as a companion (let alone his utility for the duty for which he was first brought into this world), and as such he accompanies the carriage when its owner goes out for a drive; for his fondness for horses is scarcely excelled by that of the spotted coach dog or Dalmatian. He is an excellent guard or watch, too; is not too demonstrative in his affections, and easily learns to distinguish between a friend and a foe. In the country (as in town) he is seen to advantage, for where a terrier naturally takes to hunting the rabbits and other game that may be about, the collie will not do so unless he be urged and encouraged in such delinquencies. It must, however, be said that he, like frail humanity, is easily led away from the straight and honest path, and no great pains need be taken to transform him into a confirmed poacher. Constant association with his superiors has improved his temper immensely, and the general disposition of the collie now, as compared with what it was thirty years or more ago, is much changed. Then he would rush out of the farm-yard, sniff at you, turn away, and as you did likewise you were reminded that the dog had not gone far by feeling his teeth enter the calf of one of your legs. He does not do this sort of thing now. If he is ill-natured, and he seldom is, his vice is done more openly, and he will seize his supposed foe from the front rather than from behind.

I have always been at a loss to account for this improvement in the collie's temper, and it can only have arisen from his more extended association with the general public. He is, indeed, seldom seen sulky and surly—he may be sedate, but he is ever ready to appreciate a kind word or a pat on the head; and even when kept in the country, where he seldom sees anyone but his master, his bark on the appearance of a stranger may be oftener taken as a call of welcome than as the cry of alarm. The shepherd's dog when properly trained is as good in his work now as at any previous period of his history; better, perhaps. It must not, however, be taken for granted that the collie, as he is now seen obtaining valuable prizes at our canine exhibitions, is the exact counterpart of the dog met with on the sheep-farms, and without whom the shepherd could not do his work. There are distinctions between the two. The former has been kept for his beauty alone, and most likely for generations his ancestors had never known what it was to assist the farmer in his duties. So his descendants gradually drop out of the work, and when they come to be trained are not nearly so docile and intelligent as they would have been had all their progenitors been good workers.

A young pointer or setter will often intuitively stand game on the very first occasion he may scent it, a faculty which has been handed down to him from generation to generation from dogs which have always been trained to do the same thing. A retriever puppy for a similar reason is never happy unless he is carrying something in his mouth. Neglect to keep up this seeming intuition in the pointer, setter, or retriever, and see what the result will be in the course of a few generations? The puppy will no longer point or draw upon game naturally, and his education will be ten times as difficult to consummate as it would have been had the old conditions been continued.

Thus it is with the modern exhibition-bred collie as compared with the one that has been kept and reared for work alone, and produced from parents whose capabilities and excellences in this respect have been of the highest. We occasionally see at the various trials with sheep held in different parts of the country, a rather handsome dog that is a fairly good worker, but such is the exception, and I am sorry to write that, so far as shepherding is concerned with the collie—the handsomest dogs are usually the worst workers, at any rate in public. Some exhibitors will tell you how splendidly trained to sheep or cattle their prize-winners are, but if they be so, such performances do not appear in public. Attendances for many years at some of the principal trials have led me to form this opinion. Indeed, on occasions, the duty has devolved upon me of awarding a special prize for the handsomest dog that has worked his sheep to the satisfaction of the judges, and such prizes, excepting in one or two instances that may be alluded to later on, have always gone to dogs that could not have obtained more than a h.c. card at any dog show in the kingdom. There are cases where good-looking dogs, bred from prize-winners on the bench, have been entered on the off chance of the judges allowing them to compete for the "beauty prize," irrespective of their work in the field; but the latter is generally so bad that the exhibition-bred animal is not allowed to enter the ring at the end of the day when this special honour is to be awarded.

Of course I do not mean to infer that the handsome prize winner will not work at all, my contention merely being that he cannot perform his duty so well through lack of opportunity in his progenitors, as the more common-place creature whose ancestors have spent all their lives amongst the flocks. A properly-bred collie will take to his work as naturally as a sporting dog will take to his; and I very much regret that the Collie Club has not done as much for the working capacity of its idol as it has towards beautifying and improving his appearance. Some of the very best working shepherds' dogs I have ever seen have been small, light-limbed animals, active and fleet, owning intelligent faces, and with such short wiry coats as to lead one to suspect a not very remote cross of the terrier which the farmer has kept to assist in destroying the rats, or to help the huntsman when he brings his scratch hounds round to make a raid upon the foxes. At the trials, the smooth-coated dogs, as a rule, more nearly approach show bench form than do their rough-jacketed cousins, for speed and endurance are required rather than long woolly coats, huge "frills," and "brushes" big enough to disgrace the best that ever hung behind the boldest of bold reynards.

## CHAPTER III.

EARLY SHOWS—THE FIRST CLASSES FOR SHEEP DOGS—
THE WINNERS THEREIN—GREAT DOGS, "COCKIE,"
"CHARLEMAGNE," "RUTLAND," &c. — NOTABLE
KENNELS—HIGH PRICES.

THE first dog show ever held took place at Newcastle in 1859, but, being confined entirely to pointers and setters, no class for sheep dogs or collies was provided. Although this earliest of exhibitions of the kind was on such a small scale, with a matter of sixty entries, it proved so popular and successful that it was followed by others in various parts of the country, and in November of the same year the first Birmingham show took place. That at Newcastle had been held in June, and was chiefly organised by Mr. Richard Brailsford, who likewise was responsible for the one in the Midlands. The latter was again confined to sporting dogs. Then in 1860 the prize-list came to be considerably extended, non-sporting dogs were included, and here came the first class for sheep dogs ever arranged for the show bench, dogs and bitches of all strains competing together.

The farmer at that time knew little of the value of his

dog outside his own fold, and Laddie, or whatever his name might be, had not then developed an eminence as a "fashionable beauty," a distinction which was attained later on; little wonder then that this first shepherds' dog class was a small one—five entries all told. The judging was undertaken by Mr. W. Lort, who is still to be found, as brisk and skilful as ever, awarding honour in the ring to either horses or dogs, and by the late Mr. J. H. Walsh ("Stonehenge"). In the end but one prize was awarded, it going to what was called a "pure Scotch bitch," exhibited by Mr. W. Wakefield, of Hurley, Warwickshire, who thus had the honour of taking the first show bench prize ever offered for a shepherd's dog. Two others of the entries were Scotch, collies shall I write, but the word was not in common use even then, excepting in Scotland and nearer the borders. The remaining exhibits were called English sheepdogs.

How different this one class for the variety thirty years ago from the ten that were provided in 1889—five entries then, one hundred and six now. But at Liverpool show, held during January, 1890, the entry for collies reached the extraordinary number of 245, owing, no doubt, to the excellent classification provided. There were, however, not that number of individual dogs benched, as several of the animals competed in more than one class. Still the figures show what strides in public estimation this dog has made during the last three decades.

For some time immediately following 1860 shepherd's dogs did not form a leading feature at any of the shows, and ten years later, Birmingham could only boast of an entry of fourteen, when a dog, that I consider one of the very best of the variety ever shown, took second honours.

This was Cockie, then shown by Mr. W. White, Sherwood Rise, near Nottingham, of which more anon. The first Newcastle show was followed by others, and in 1864 a class for sheep dogs in the county town of Northumberland secured eight entries, two of the exhibitors being Mr. James Hedley, the well-known greyhound coursing judge, and Mr. Jacob Wilson (now Sir Jacob Wilson), so well known by his work in connection with the Royal Agricultural Society.

Hanley, in Staffordshre, was responsible for a good provincial show in 1868, and amongst the nine sheep-dogs benched were two by the Rev. W. J. Mellor, and by Mr. R. J. Lloyd Price, of Rhiwlas. The first named took leading honours with his dog, which had not a name, but Mr. Price was not so fortunate. Another exhibitor, who survives, could show and win in this class so long ago as 1863, viz., Mr. T. Wootten, whose old, heavy-coated, characteristic, if rather coarse headed dog, Rover, came second at Birmingham that year, and in the following one likewise; Mr. Greaves, M.P., of Barford, Warwickshire, winning first on both occasions, with a dog called Yarrow.

Between this period and 1870 the London and provincial shows, the latter especially, secured fairly large entries when classes were given for sheep dogs; and it was during this decade that such exhibitions became popularised, and at the same time the dogs that made them attracted more than passing attention. In 1868 Darlington took the initiative, and duplicated the class by giving one for dogs and one for bitches, there being twenty-four entries in the one and seven in the other. A strange anomaly appears here, not an error as it has been considered, but merely a local custom, the males were called "shepherds' dogs," the females "cur bitches." In many parts of the country the cognomen still remains with the shepherds' dogs, although not restricted to the one sex, and cur dog and cur bitch are by no means of unusual application anywhere north of the Trent. The term "cur" is neither a nice one, nor complimentary to so noble a breed of dog as that of the shepherds', for he is by no means that ignoble and worthless variety such an ill-chosen name implies.

Two years later, viz., in 1870, the Darlington management came again to the fore by providing a challenge class which was for both dogs and bitches; the open one was likewise for dogs and bitches rough coated, and now for about the first time was a special class provided for the smooth coated variety. The latter, very numerous in north Yorkshire, Durham, and Northumberland, useful active dogs both on the hill and fell sides, and on the leveller and lower-lying pastures. Five champions were forward, twenty-five rough coated dogs and bitches, and fifteen smooth coated ones.

So much for the progress of classes, and most of the dogs that were winners up to twenty years ago are well-nigh forgotten. Rovers and Laddies were in force — eight of the former and eleven of the latter appear in the first volume of the Stud Book—and few now recollect Mr. Palhorpe's Rover, Mr. Gamon's Laddie, Mr. John Inman's Samson, Mr. J. Ashcroft's Rob, or Mr. J. Smith's Rover, all great, good dogs in their day, prize-winners, and the best of their race at that time.

Most of these were rather heavy, cumbersome animals, generally black and tan in colour, sometimes grey or dull brown or mixed brindle sable, the bright red or orange tints being scarcely known then. Mr. Inman's dog did a considerable amount of winning at local shows, and he was a thorough type of a collie, which I fancy would be useful to cross with the somewhat effeminate-headed animals so popular now. Black and tan in colour, with little white about him, his coat was dense and close underneath, harder on the surface; he was a big dog, with moderate ears, rather slow in his movements, a little sour in his expression, but with a skull and face that denoted more than ordinary intelligence, a stamp of animal more likely to be useful as an assistant to the drover rather than to the shepherd. As a fact, the best of these early-day sheep dogs were picked up by their exhibitors in the cattle-markets of our country and larger towns, whither the farmers and dealers had brought them with their sheep or other live stock. They had been bred without any idea as to pedigree, and when anything more than usually good looking came to be produced such was rather by reason of good luck than otherwise.

Allusion has already been made to that excellent dog "Cockie," from whom are descended almost all the best collies of the present day, and what old Jock and Old Trap were in fox terriers, old Cockie was certainly in sheep dogs, well nigh the progenitor of the present race of his variety. History does not tell us where he was bred. The Kennel Club Stud-book makes pretence of doing so, but it is quite as wrong in printing that he was bred by Mr. W. H. Johnson, of Eccles, as it is in stating (a gross printer's error) that he was born in 1368! Mr. W. White was the first man who showed the dog, which he did with an extraordinary amount of thoroughly deserved success, for Cockie was certainly by far the best dog of his day, and were he as young and fit now as when I saw him win in a large class at Carlisle in 1870, there is no dog to-day who could fairly and squarely beat him. Some judges might put him back, but they would be his vanquishers and not those of his own tribe opposed to him. As a fact, at the Carlisle show in question, he was the only dog that had been winning prizes this side the border that the judges noticed, and they were farmers and agriculturists who had never seen Cockie before, and made their awards from his appearance of a likelihood for work more than from his beauty alone. The dog could receive no higher testimonial than this, and those Carlisle farmers pronounced him by far the best collie dog they had ever seen.

Cockie was a brown sable and white in colour, the brown shading considerably mixed with darker coloured hair. His legs and feet were of the best, so was his coat, though, perhaps, modern admirers of the woolly jacket would take exception to the hardness, denseness, and slight waviness in Cockie's. He had a strong back, well muscled loins, nice stern, well carried, and his head and expression were perfect; so were his ears small and well carried, though in the photograph from which the engraving at the commencement of this volume was made, the ears are thrown back into the hair on the neck. This is the type of collie that should be produced now. He was good all round, without exaggeration in any particular feature. Cockie only became the property of Mr. Johnson when past his best, and was kept by that gentlemen as a sensible companion, and no dog was more so; but the poor old fellow developed an obesity in his later days which quite spoiled his shape, and resulted in a loss of coat and general form much to be deplored. However, he left some good sons and daughters behind him when he died in August, 1882, in the possession of Mr. J. Bissell,

Birmingham, cared for and cherished as so excellent a dog deserved. Prior to the whilom champion obtaining sanctuary at Great Bars he was sold by auction in one of the local repositories, realising but three pounds or so. Mr. Bissell repurchased him for £10. The best dog of his day bringing to a close his public life in a manner similar to that in which a few years later, another almost equally celebrated sheep dog commenced his career.

I take Cockie's best performance to be that at Carlisle, but he was repeatedly seen winning either first or second honours at Birmingham, always being defeated by inferior animals. At Nottingham, in 1872, he could only come second to Mr. Holmes's Bob, a black and tan, if I remember aright; and Mr. Henry Lacy's Mec beat him at Birmingham one year, but on another occasion the tables were turned. This last-named dog was a great winner in his day, and must have had a curious career. He, like Cockie, had no reliable pedigree, but, unlike his superior, was a black and tan dog, peculiarly good in head, ears, and general form, but soft in coat, and rather deficient in brightness of expression. Mec first came into notice at a small show held at Bedford Leigh, in Lancashire, where he was purchased for about £3 by the late Mr. John Henshall, of Salford, the writer being present, and a witness to the bargain at the time. Bulldogs were, however, more in Mr. Henshall's line than collies, so in due course Mec, for a consideration, was transferred to the kennels of Mr. Henry Lacy, of Hebden Bridge, then a constant frequenter of dog shows, and at the same time a most successful exhibitor. For him Mec won many prizes, and proved fairly useful as a stud dog.

Another celebrity about this time was Mr. Christopher

W. Wilson's Malcolm, a peculiarly richly-coloured black and tan dog, purchased for a few pounds at Penrith show, I think, in 1870. Again is there no pedigree, and considerable confusion is made in his entry in the first volume of the Stud Book. Malcolm was a fair dog only, when compared with an animal like Cockie—his temper was not so amiable as it might have been, and he carried his stern in somewhat Pomeranian-like fashion, curled into his back. He might have been a success at the stud: I have seen excellent dogs by him, but, unfortunately, when in his prime there was a nonsensical idea that the black and tan sheepdogs obtained their colour through crossing with the Gordon setter. There is no doubt the contrary was the case, and that the Gordon setter had his coat and sensibility improved by being crossed with the Highland sheep dog. Black and white, black and tan, and black, white, and tan were the real Scotch collie colours before the gaudier and handsomer reds, yellows, or browns (now known as sables) were produced. If Malcolm did not prove so great a success as he might have done had he lived in less vilifying times, the prizes he won for his owner induced a fondness for the show ring which culminated in Mr. Wilson obtaining a world-wide celebrity as the breeder of many of the best hackneys and ponies of the day.

Coming a year or two later than the three already described notabilities, was Mr. S. E. Shirley's Shamrock, a tri-coloured showily-marked dog in black, white, and tan, and one not much after my fancy owing to a peculiar softness in his expression, even amounting to silliness, which, in one or two cases he, unfortunately, transmitted to his offspring, and his coat was not of a good texture. Strangely, this dog came from the north of Ireland, but no

E

doubt his immediate ancestors sprung from Scotland, and his sire is given as Mr. Call's Shep, his dam being Mr. C. Glasby's Bess. Shamrock had more than his fair share of show honours during 1873, and following him from the same kennel came Tricolour, Trefoil, and Hornpipe, the latter possibly the best of the batch the popular chairman of the Kennel Club has shown. The strain of Mr. Shirley's dogs is in the main responsible for almost all the good collies now winning on the bench, for his Trefoil was the sire of Charlemagne, whose successes at the stud have been quite equal to those of any sire that either preceded or has followed him. Charlemagne's dam was Maud, a daughter of Cockie. No doubt, this continuity of type handed down from the Trefoil and Shamrock strains, points to their purity in the first instance, and one may almost wonder what our present collies would have been like had the above strains, and their distinguished ancestor, old Cockie, never had an existence.

One of this strain (Highlander, by Cockie—Hulakin), now the property of Mr. T. Easton, Storrs Farm, Windermere, when a puppy was purchased by Mr. T. Bassett from Mr. Shirley for about £80—a long price in those days, but which a few years later came to be exceeded on many occasions. Highlander is one of the wearing sort. He is as good now at eight years old as when he was a young dog, not one of the narrow-headed contingent—a thorough collie in every way, with a protective jacket; but his ears are not always carried in quite orthodox fashion. In his time he begat a very good dog in Rob Roy Macgregor, from that exceedingly well-bred bitch, Hasty, by Carlyle—Glen. Rob Roy Macgregor was a handsome tricolour, black, white, and tan, a strong, heavy dog, a useful rather than an ornamental sort, and one that did not remain long upon the show bench.

Prior to the era of the two last-named dogs, other notabilities were to the fore, one named Carlyle, a big sable, first shown by Mr. Skidmore, of Nantwich; later by Dr. James and Mr. Ashwen, creating quite a sensation by reason of the great length of his head and face. His ears were bad, so was his type, and the unusual length of his head was owing to the fact of his being very much "pig-jawed, *i.e.*, the upper jaw and teeth projected in front of the lower, a deformity in my eyes, but one which did not appear to keep him out of the prize lists. So he was bred from, and may be responsible in some degree for the narrow heads that are so far from uncommon in this year of grace 1890. A better dog than this was old Hero. I think the same that was shown by Mr. E. Oldroyd, so early as 1873, and the almost black Marcus, which Mr. W. W. Thomson had imported from Scotland (Carlyle's home), was far above the average—a collie, in fact, if a little short in the neck and rather loaded at his shoulders.

This was a stamp of dog of a kind often admired on the benches at the Edinburgh and Glasgow shows, and time after time such were found winning chief prizes. Personally, I regret the almost total extinction of these black and black and white specimens, many of them having white collars or frills, white breasts, and white at the tips of their tails. Such were usually useful-looking dogs for work, not too low on their legs, nor with a superabundance of coat. Their feet were thick and tight, their activity could not be surpassed, and in correct expression and character they were not excelled by the best of the more modern strains. Some specimens of the latter might beat these black and whites in smallness of ear, but in nothing else; and does not Burns tell us the collie should be black and white? One of the best of these came south, a bitch named Time, which George Stables, now kennelman to Sir Humphrey de Trafford, claimed at one of the Scottish shows for something like £15. She was an excellent bitch in every way, and, so far as show was concerned, must have proved remunerative to her exhibitor.

Another of these white and blacks, a heavier stamp though than Time, ran well at the Westmoreland trials some years later, viz., in 1883, and in the end won the cup presented by Lady Bective for the handsomest dog on the ground, whose work had proved satisfactory. This dog, Sir William, direct from Scotland, was the property of the shepherd on the Storrs Farm, on the banks of Windermere, and had not had special training for the Field Trial work. The only animal approaching this strain I know to-day in England as a winner on the bench, is that right excellent old dog Sly Fox, the property of Mr. H. Ralph (London). He is a medium-sized dog, with not very much white about him, his sire was Fox, his dam being Zulu Princess by Marcus, he of course inheriting the black blood on his dam's side. This cross of the sables with the blacks—for Fox was of the sable strain, being by Charlemagne—appears to have been fairly successful, for the owner of Sly Fox, whenever he be inclined to put his dogs on the show bench, has something above an average to be seen, What's Wanted and Johnny Norman usually being there or thereabouts in the prize-list. Sly Fox has done a considerable amount of winning, and is at the present time eligible to compete in the champion classes.

In such a summary as this it is not quite advisable to

keep a correct chronological order, so continuing with modern times the successful epoch of Mr. James Bissell is reached. I suppose from 1878 to about 1884 Mr. Bissell had almost his own way in the matter of collies, for by judicious mating and careful breeding he obtained a strain, the best specimens of which were at that time quite invincible. A sable dog called Wolf, another son of Cockie's, from Lorna, by Tartan—Maud, was his first great success, and with him he won at Birmingham in 1879, also securing chief honours in the bitch class with Flirt, and the champion prize with another bitch called Lorna. All these were good animals, but in the open dog class was a puppy shown, and he got V.H.C., that was destined to make a great name in the canine world and attain chief honours at Curzon Hall for five years in succession. This was the well-known Charlemagne, considered by many good judges to be the best collie of all times; I considered him inferior to Cockie, though no doubt the handsomer animal of the two—more of the drawing-room dog in fact.

Charlemagne is a clear sable and white in colour, with beautifully placed and exquisitely-carried ears; his coat is profuse, close, and of prime texture; his bone is good, his fore legs and feet of the best; he might with advantage have more powerful loins, and he is rather cow-hocked, a defect that increasing years intensified. His expression, docile and amiable, is a little lacking fire, but as bright and intellectual as Nature could produce on any dog. He was, however, a dog of a generation, and from 1880 to 1884 inclusive, during the Birmingham show week, Mr. Bissell's favourite might have been seen holding quite a levee and behaving himself well under the circumstances. This dog lasted well because he was not overshown, and he was not beaten in his champion class at Birmingham until the black and tan dog Rutland was placed over him in 1885. After being kept at home for a time one was somewhat taken aback to find the old dog, notwithstanding the eleven years and more through which he had lived, occupying the first bench in the last show of the Collie Club, held in Holborn in February, 1890. Yes! there he was, surrounded by spectators as usual, grizzled and grey somewhat, yet retaining his old form and character in an extraordinary manner. He had grown more like his grand sire Cockie than ever. His coat was thick and dense as ever, crispish, too, a good warm jacket if a little too curly for modern tastes. He had little to beat in the department of veterans he so well graced, but when the contest for the sixty guinea challenge cup came on, in which he had to compete against all the prize winners in the show, matters, were different. He was not smart and brisk in the ring. How could he be so? Still, the judge, Mr. Wake-Walker, placed him over all, because he considered him best in every way excepting so far as locomotion was concerned.

Many bold bids of good money have been made for Charlemagne, and at times dogs of much the same blood were claimed at what must be considered exorbitant prices, the little sable dog Eclipse to wit, which Mr. W. W. Thomson secured at Birmingham, on behalf of Mr. George Krehl, for £100. This was a nice dog all round, too bitch-like though, and by no means a bargain for the hundred pound note, though no doubt in one way and another his owner made him a remunerative speculation. Eclipse was a dog of charming disposition and much sense, and no one need desire a handsomer dog as a companion, for which purpose the Scotch Collie has gradually drifted southwards from a northern home amid fern and heather, with a bed in a corner of his master's plaid, left hanging loose for the purpose. Is he happier in his new abode? forms a question the dog could only answer for himself—that he is better fed because more valued pecuniarily, there can be no doubt. But gentle walking exercise in the bustling thoroughfare of our large centres must have come as a great change to his unlimited galloping and exercising ground on the northern hills. Possibly, with the dog as with the man, what the eye does not see the heart does not grieve for.

There is an interesting history attached to the next notable collie dog I shall mention—a history so unique, so peculiar throughout, that one is led to express astonishment at the occurrence of such a thing in these enlightened times, when the knowledge of the good points of a dog is said to be possessed by every man. We hear of *ci-devant* Derby and Leger favourites ending their days between the shafts of a hansom or in the knacker's yard; here we have the case of a dog whose fortune varied even to a greater extent. The Rev. Hans Hamilton had a black and tan puppy which he presented to Mr. S. E. Shirley, who in turn handed it over to Sir Charles Mordaunt, who, unfortunately, did not bring up the dog in the paths of honesty, and, not contented with roaming over the demesne of Sir Charles, it strayed apace, and chased the sheep on a neighbouring farm. For this crime he was sentenced to be transported, and, in part exchange for a rather noted prize winner called Staffa, became the property of Mr. Walker, of Warwick. That gentleman did not fancy the budding champion much, so sent him over to the Birmingham Repository, where such things are sold, and here, for fifty shillings, the dog became the property of Mr. Emery, a collie exhibitor and an admirer of the gentle race. We next see the dog in a selling class at Gloucester, where, attracting the eye of Mr. S. Boddington, of Birmingham, he was claimed for £5. In four months more, that astute judge having christened his new purchase Rutland, showed him to such advantage that the dog had become a champion, was recognised as about the best of his variety before the public, and as such was eventually sold to Mr. A. H. Megson, of Manchester for, it is said, £250. Cockie had been purchased in one of the markets in the Midlands for a couple of pounds. Mec, another champion, was picked up for little more than that sum, and here we have a third pillar of the collie world once given away, then sold for fifty shillings, eventually to find a purchaser and a happy home for the extraordinary sum of £250, for which quite a flock of very good sheep could be obtained. Do not prices such as these prove some indication that the farmer, in these times of agricultural depression, might add to his revenue by endeavouring to breed Rutlands, Mecs, and Cockies. Surely, if he could not produce animals quite of their value he might be able to obtain specimens worth £10 or £20; at any rate, conducted on a small scale, breeding from good strains of the collie would be much more remunerative than poultry keeping and fruit culture on a large scale.

Rutland, a medium-sized dog, of black and tan colour, without any white tag or collar to relieve the two shades, was not quite so attractive to the eye as gaudier markings would have made him. Still, he was a dog of that good class that the more you looked at him the better he pleased, and, indeed, there was little fault to be found with him, although personally he would have pleased better had he stood a little higher on his legs and possessed more character in his expression. His coat, head, ears, and general shape were tip top, and these, with his other good qualities, he in many cases managed to impress upon his sons and daughters, and "Rutland blood" is still much in request.

Before, however, proceeding with the strains that bring one rapidly right up to the present time, something must be said about Mr. M. C. Ashwin's Cocksie, a dog that has often been confused, owing to the resemblance in name, with his sire Cockie. As I write, Cocksie is still fresh and well, though fourteen years old this very day (February 16th), and he has never been out of the hands of his present owner, who bred him from Lassie, a winning bitch without pedigree, a brown sable and white in colour. Cocksie was remarkable for his extraordinarily profuse coat, of good quality, which he still retains. He was a good all-round dog, but not quite equal to his sire in character and expression, though he won a large number of first prizes at the leading shows, being twice second at Birmingham, in 1879, beating Charlemagne, and on several occasions he was placed at the head of affairs at the London shows of the Kennel Club. It is thirteen years since Cocksie won his first prize, a gold medal, presented by Mr. Panmure Gordon for the best collie at the Islington show, 1877, which had never previously won a prize.

So long-lived a dog as this favourite of Mr. Ashwin's, naturally carries us over a great many years, and is, indeed, a connecting link with the past and present generations. Much-exhibited dogs are not long-lived, some eight years or so being, as a rule, the limit of their span, and seldom do they retain their good looks to take a premier position for more than two or three years, some few animals already mentioned being quite exceptions to the rule.

Although one has considerable fault to find with many of the collies that are now taking prizes, especially as being unfitted for their legitimate work, there is no doubt that at the present time there are more really good specimens in the country than at any previous time of our history. A dozen or two first-class animals could readily be mentioned. There are many good judges of the variety, but a far greater number of individuals who take a pride in breeding them to pattern, or as near to pattern as possible.

The Rev. Hans Hamilton has for years been a most successful exhibitor with dogs of his own breeding, his Captain, Peggie II., Dorothy, Woodmansterne Lothian (who unfortunately succumbed to distemper before he had reached that position on the show bench to which he would have attained) with others already mentioned—all being noteworthy. Mr. Hamilton has, I believe, on more than one occasion, had the honour of presenting his collies to Her Majesty, a privilege likewise granted to the Messrs. Charles, neighbours of Mr. Ashwin, already alluded to, near Stratford-on-Avon. The latter gentlemen, time after time, introduced some of our best specimens to the public, and made a speciality of producing occasional dogs almost white in colour—handsome and unique as companions, but not so useful for working purposes as others less like the sheep themselves. Possibly, their best dog was the Squire, whose defect lay in a deficiency of coat, recently sold to America for a large sum—as was Bendigo, a son of his, a most promising puppy that does not seem to have realised early anticipations of excellence. Some of Messrs. Charles' bitches were particularly good, the lovely rich red sable Bertha being, to my idea, the best of her sex on the bench for about two years; she, however, like the Squire, did not grow a profuse coat, but what there was of it was of excellent texture. Earlier than this Messrs. Charles had the privilege of bringing out that excellent bitch Flurry.

Mr. J. J. Steward, of near Rugby, has also been a successful breeder, and he may well claim to have the honour of introducing the most sensational collie puppy on record. This young dog (Caractacus) was sensational in many ways: the difference of opinion as to his merits and the extraordinary price for which he was sold at Liverpool show in 1888. He was there entered in the catalogue at £100, and, after winning first prize in the puppy class under Mr. C. H. Wheeler, the officiating judge, was claimed by several individuals who admired the dog. The latter being the case, the fortunate puppy was put up to auction with the result that he did not become the property of Mr. Megson, of Manchester, until £350 had been bid! Caractacus, then nine months old, sickened from distemper, after the show, but, fortunately, did not succumb thereto as many good dogs have done, and will do again.

Now for a description of this extraordinary puppy. He is a grey sable in colour, with a little white—an ugly colour, in fact, and his appearance is by no means improved by a couple of very light-coloured eyes. He is a big dog, weighing about 64lb., standing on the best of legs and feet, with power both in front and behind, and his coat is good, so are his ears, and there is no fault to be found with the shape of his head. His detractors contend that his expression is all wrong, arising, no doubt, from his colour, and the lightness of his eyes, and that he moves stiffly, and would be little use as a sheepdog at all so far as work is concerned. I cannot say they are wrong, and, so far as appearances are concerned, Caractacus was as high priced as he was dear. Mr. Megson has, in his kennel, some better dogs than this, including the particularly handsome Metchley Wonder (of which an engraving appears facing page 66), for which rumour says he paid Mr. S. Boddington £530! This is a handsome sable and white dog, of medium size, probably 55lb. or so in weight, and with generally little fault to be found with him, excepting one would like to have seen a broader skull that would have given an appearance of greater intelligence in the face than Wonder presents at present; still, his exceedingly perfect legs and feet, excellent body, strong and muscular hind quarters, in combination with other fine attributes, stamp him as one of the best of his variety hitherto introduced to the public, and he promises to even excel such notabilities as Cockie and Charlemagne in transmitting his good qualities to his family. Another great dog in the same kennels is Edgbaston Fox, likewise sable and white in colour, bred by Mr. A. L. Chance, and by him shown as Great Alne Skye. All these later dogs have pedigrees, and most of them possess much the same blood as those Mr. Bissell won so much with, and descended from Cockie and Mr. Shirley's strains, which have been mentioned earlier on.

In some respects Mr. W. Arkwright, of Sutton Scarsdale, possesses the most unique kennel of collies, as for years he has given his attention to produce them of the mirled or marbled colour, with china or wall eyes. This peculiar hue was oftener found amongst the smooth-coated variety than in the rough-haired division; but occasionally there cropped up in the latter a mirled specimen of more than usual excellence. I think that it was at Dundee show, in 1880, that the judge (Mr. Hugh Dalziel) placed a dog of this colour (Mr. G. L. Lowe's Tweed) at the top of a very fair class, which included Trevor and Highlander, and the same judge, at a smaller exhibition at Fakenham, in Kent, selected another of the same variety, Mr. Brackenridge's Scott, for premier honours. Such dogs as those were more or less flukes, but, by judicious crossing, Mr. Arkwright breeds these mirled specimens almost to order. On many occasions such have been successfully exhibited, and his dog (Blue Sky) and his bitch (Blue Ruin) were particularly good specimens, the latter the best bitch of her year. Mr. Arkwright, in the spring of this year, sold all his collies at Aldridge's, Blue Ruin being purchased for 99 guineas by Mr. Panmure Gordon.

From Westmorland Dr. James, Kirkby Lonsdale, one of the oldest exhibitors and best of judges, at times introduces some dog or bitch of unusual excellence. Indeed, for some years this gentleman has, perhaps, given more attention and devoted more time than anyone else in his attempts to produce the proper article. But breeding even dogs is almost as uncertain as breeding shorthorns, and a man must be both lucky and clever to obtain specimens anything like approaching perfection. He owned the well-known Trevor by Trefoil—Maud by Cockie, for a long time, a dog with great character in every way but in his stern, which he preferred to carry right over his back, although good training and the judicious use of a stick when in the ring altered matters considerably, and the brush was carried with a downward curve. Trevor was an oddly-coloured dog, it being a matter of opinion whether he was a black and tan or very dark sable. Some, who were not colour-blind, held to the former, and others, with equal claim to such knowledge, held quite opposite opinions.

Now, the little dog Scotforth, from the same kennels, that he has shown lately, would be about perfection had he absolutely straight fore legs, and were he a size larger. In character and true collie attributes I believe he can easily beat any of his contemporaries—he fails where I have said. Marigold and White Heather are also lovely bitches; the latter has worn a little lately, and in a degree lost her bloom. When fit and well she was one of the best of her sex that ever graced the bench—the equal of Messrs. Charles's Bertha, mentioned earlier on. Both these were better than some of the so-called wonderful puppies (of which Pitch Dark was an example), who blaze forth, meteor-like, for a few days, are sold for exorbitant figures, and in the end sink into oblivion. A dog should be bred to last and keep his form, not to be seemingly perfect at nine months old, and when matured become as coarse and rough as a cart-horse. One often wonders what becomes of all the prize dogs, for there are few that continue such for more than twelve months, and some there are that have run their race in half that time.

Mr. T. H. Stretch, of Ormskirk, has, during the past few years, come very much to the fore as exhibitor and breeder, and to him and to the Rev. Hans Hamilton are due, in a great measure, the gaudier-coloured strains of the collie now so often seen. The dog that won in the open class at Liverpool this year (1890), Christopher, bred by Mr. Hamilton, owned by Mr. Stretch, is one of our best animals of his variety, neither too big nor too little—a useful size, indeed, with a workmanlike and sensible appearance, with the addition of beauty in colouring and coat; his ears, too, are very good. Following his success at Liverpool, at the Collie Club show held at the end of February, Christopher was placed over his sire, Metchley Wonder, for the challenge prize, and there attracted the attention of Mr. Mitchell Harrison, of the United States. In due course a bargain was struck, Christopher changing hands for £700 in cash and two other dogs, Dublin Scott and Charleroi II., valued at £150 apiece, so it may be said that the extraordinary price of £1000 was given for this handsome son of Peggie II. This is by far the highest price ever paid for a purely fancy dog, excepting for a St. Bernard; such a sum has seldom been given for a greyhound, and never for a pointer, setter, or any other sporting dog, excepting in the case of a greyhound. Ormskirk Amazement is by many judges considered the dog of the day—I believe there are at least half-a-dozen living now, in March, 1890, that can beat him. He is handsome in colour and markings, possesses extraordinary coat and frill, is a nice-sized symmetrical dog, and his ears are all right. To many he is attractive by the extraordinary length of his head, produced by his upper jaw and teeth projecting very much in front of the lower ones. He is sadly "over-shot," or "pig-jawed," and how far this defect is to be taken into consideration judges must consider when making their awards. Some of the bitches from the Ormskirk kennel are likewise amazingly excellent, including Ormskirk Dolly, first at Birmingham, in 1889, where she was claimed by Mr. Percy Heaton, at the catalogue price of £100. At the next big show, which came off at Liverpool, with her name changed to Keepsake, she was, however, beaten by a bitch bred by

Mr. F. Hurst, Knutsford, and shown by Mr. J. Rankin, Scotland, called "Bleachfield Wonder," whose sire is Metchley Wonder, and dam Britannia by Rutland. This female wonder was as good in every particular as Dolly, and bigger to boot; and such being Mr. Heaton's opinion she went into his kennel and won for her new owner almost immediately.

Another successful exhibitor and frequent judge is Mr. C. H. Wheeler, of Birmingham, who has a happy knack of buying a dog for a small sum and selling it for a large one; but, in addition to this, he has bred some very good sheep dogs, and claims to be one of the oldest admirers of this now fashionable breed. A man must be a good judge to be able to buy a dog for a few half-crowns, and then sell it for as many pounds; but I am rather doubtful whether such procedure is quite the proper method to take with a view of improving any breed. The best dogs Mr. Wheeler has possessed have been Malcolm I., Edgbaston Fox, sold for £250, Lorna Doon, Sir Noel, and Edgbaston Victor.

Although in Scotland there are no such celebrated kennels as this country has provided, there have been a few extra good specimens of the collie from the Land o' Cakes, still, as already hinted, the lovely black and white specimens, so often found there, have had their places usurped by the southern invaders of brighter hues. Not long ago, at one of the Edinburgh shows in Waverley Market, I thought I had found an extraordinarily good collie of real Scotch breeding, a special one in every way. On referring to the catalogue I became disillusioned, for this dog (Tarquin, Mr. T. Gilholm's) had for his sire our old English champion, Rutland. This Tarquin, albeit of evil temper, is, perhaps, the best of his class that has been produced over the border, although he was not fortunate enough to win the head prize on that occasion, when my attention was drawn to him. He is a sable dog, of an excellent type in every way, but, perhaps, not long enough nor narrow enough in his head to suit everyone.

Miss L. Harvey, of Blackruthven, near Perth, is, perhaps, the most successful of all Scottish exhibitors of their national dog, her Roderick of Ruthven and Belle of Ruthven, with other winners, being a credit to any kennels, and only likely to be beaten by the very best of their class. Then, at Glenboig, Mr. R. Chapman has, time after time, bred some excellent dogs, and, no doubt, would have done better had he not given so much of his attention to the sporting varieties, of which he has such good store. *Apropos* just here, I may say that Mr. Chapman has an almost unique lot of Gordon setters; but the world has yet to learn that he keeps them for the production of special black and tan collies. Another generation the two varieties may be coupled as being in the same kennel, and some learned historian jump to the conclusion that they were bred together from the same parents. Mr. H. Nimmo, Wishaw, and Mr. B. R. Haigh, Portobello, are likewise noted Scottish admirers and exhibitors of the collie.

The first prize dog in the open class at Birmingham in 1889 must, however, appear as a Scotch dog, though his sire be Christopher, already named, and his dam only semi-Gaelic in pedigree. Mr. Morton Campbell, of Huntley Hill, Brechin, owns the dog in question, Stracathro Ralph, who was but a little over fourteen months old when he secured the high honour, which he followed up a few months afterwards by winning the valuable challenge trophy as the best dog at Liverpool Show under eighteen months old. On the latter occasion he was beaten in his class by his sire. Stracathro Ralph is a medium-sized dog of the fashionable sable and white colour, fairly uniform in quality throughout, without any predominating excellence in any one particular. His coat is of good quality and perfectly straight; his ears might be improved, and so might his expression, and he gives one the idea of being the kind of dog likely to develop a cobbiness and shortness in back with increasing age. Nevertheless, though a very good dog indeed, I considered him inferior to Mr. Chance's Great Alne Douglas, a bigger and stronger dog than Ralph, though he does not as a rule carry so much coat. This notwithstanding, he beats Mr. Campbell's dog in character and expression, and in my opinion, at the time this is being written, there is not a collie living that I have seen, and almost all the best have come before me at one time or another, that can on all points beat Mr. Chance's well-bred son of Metchley Wonder and Sweet Fanny. His portrait is given on the adjoining page.

Another successful breeder is Mr. H. C. While of Sutton Coldfield, his Maney Squire and other Maneys often been seen in the prize-ring, and many besides, more than average dogs, continue being introduced. Mr. V. Kilvert's Cestrian Wonder, Mr. R. Barklie's Umba, Mr. V. T. Thompson's Tuppence; another of the best bitches, Mr. J. Pirie's Paramount, Mr. W. R. Dockrell's Flurry, Scotilla and Dublin Scott, and Mr. F. G. Oliver's Barbillon, may be specially mentioned; nor must the name of Mr. T. Mercier be omitted, who, although living in Co. Down, Ireland, is not too far away to send good specimens over to this country and take the highest honours with them.

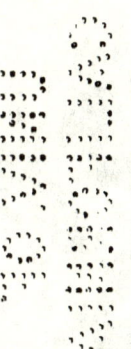

Great Alne Douglas.

Metchley Wonder.

Dr. McGill, Littleborough, near Manchester, has, during the past few years, been as ardent an admirer of the collie as he has proved a successful exhibitor. His favourites, bearing the now well known prefix of "Hollin," are usually particularly handsomely marked, and excellent in other particulars. Hollin Bitters and Pansey, successful at the late Collie Club's Show and at subsequent exhibitions, are possibly equal to anything that has appeared from the Hollin House kennels.

The Messrs. Birch, of Seaforth; Mr. Hurst, Knutsford; Mr. Wake-Walker, Watford; Lady Innes-Ker, Mr. F. Hurst, Mr. G. Hall, Mr. H. Ainscough, Mr. A. N. Radcliffe, Mr. M. H. Lowe, Mr. H. J. Clements, and the Rev. C. Kent, in addition to the gentlemen already named, have possessed some excellent strains, specimens of which have time after time been seen to advantage in the rings of many of our shows.

But their names are almost in legions who have owned prize-winning sheep dogs, for is not their variety, after the fox terrier, the most popular of the canine race? Many good dogs may have been omitted; possibly, some, in the eyes of their owners, even better than one half of those whose names appear in these pages, but the endeavour has been to select only those which I myself have seen and of whose merits I was thus able to judge. This chapter has been altogether devoted to those rough-coated shepherds' dogs that have made names for themselves, and gained notoriety for their owners, on the show bench. Further on something will be forthcoming as to the working capabilities of the collie. One may rail at the modern type and the show bench as one likes, still there is no avoiding the fact that, had it not been for the latter, and the selection of the handsomest specimens to appear thereon, the present popularity would not have been attained, and the long prices given for the best specimens must have been more imaginative than real.

Following the custom that had been inaugurated in the case of pointers and setters, our American cousins were not slow to perceive the value of the show bench collie, and many admirers of the variety were found across the Atlantic, who moreover had the wherewithal to please their fancy. This they did by making judicious purchases, and from time to time many well-bred collie dogs made the voyage, and are now located in different parts of the United States and Canada. Indeed, at the last exhibition of the Westminster Kennel Club, held in New York, in February, 1890, one hundred and seventeen collies were entered, a number well up to the average found at an ordinary show in this country.

The earliest importations of note were Marcus, Robin Adair, and Zulu Princess; but the latest of all were Christopher, already named, and that grand dog The Squire, which Mr. Mitchell Harrison purchased from Messrs. Charles for a good stiff figure. These dogs, properly mated, should have great influence in improving the breed in America. Of other notabilities that have left our shores during the past half dozen years may be named Dublin Scott, Maney Trefoil, Flurry II., and Scotilla, the spirited owner of the latter, sending him over to compete at the Kennel Club summer show in London in 1889, which he did, unfortunately, with an amount of success not commensurate with the expense entailed by so bold an undertaking. Judging from the reports in the American papers, the following gentlemen are the most prominent admirers of the collie over there; Mr. Harrison, already alluded to; Mr. T. H. Terry, Mr. J. Lindsay, Mr. W. Apgar, Mr. McEwen, Mr. Gibson, Mr. J. D. Shotwell, Mr. A. R. Kyle, and Mr. James Watson.

Notwithstanding the loss to us of so many good dogs, I do not think the time has yet approached when our own kennels here will have, as it were, to play second fiddle to dogs from the States or from any of our colonial possessions. The system of quarantine in existence in New Zealand and Australia has prevented, in a great measure, the import of shepherds' dogs to these great dependencies, and I believe that the climate has not been found suitable to such dogs as have been taken to the colonies for the purpose of assisting the farmer with his cattle and the shepherd with his flock.

## CHAPTER IV.

The Smooth-coated Collie—Where he springs from—His Varieties and Types—His Colours—Some of the best Dogs—A sagacious Bitch—Punishment of a Dog Thief.

CASUAL allusions have been made earlier on to a variety of collie the coat of which is short or smooth, an active, useful animal, valuable in all descriptions of farm work where sheep and cattle are concerned. These smooth dogs have been found most numerous and of greatest excellence in the north of England—in Durham and Northumberland especially—and although choice specimens may occasionally crop up elsewhere their parents in nine cases out of ten are found to have sprung from the counties named or the localities bordering thereon. The farmers in the Weardale district are particularly fond of this smooth-coated dog, and some of them have bred it with great care for many generations, with a result that they are produced true to type. I do not find that the advent of dog shows has improved them one iota, nor have exhibitors thereat contrived to breed specimens of this smooth variety to as high a standard of perfection as they have the long coated one. The farmer still produces the best smooth specimens, the exhibitor has the honour of doing the like so far as his cousin is concerned.

Bewick is again to the fore in giving us an engraving of the smooth collie, which he calls the "Cur," a name still attaching to the variety in many parts of the country, and, as already stated, arising from the fact that shepherds' dogs were "cur-tailed" by having their tails cut. Bewick's drawing is much of a muchness as a careful artist would make to-day of the same variety, a little more coat, perhaps, and a bigger and stronger dog than is usually considered quite *chic* by those who know the right sort to win. The dogs, though, of this variety are, as a rule, much bigger and generally coarser than the bitches, the difference between the sexes not being so marked in any variety of medium-sized canines, excepting, perhaps, in the Scotch deerhounds and, of course, in the rough-coated collies themselves.

In an earlier chapter it was stated that at the South Durham and North Yorkshire shows, held at Darlington, in July, 1870, one of the first classes for smooth-coated collies was provided, and it had a capital entry of fifteen, as many as will probably be found at the same show in 1890, so the variety has not popularised itself very much. I say one of the earliest classes, because in June of the same year prizes were offered for smooth-coated sheep dogs at the first Crystal Palace dog show, but the prizes were withheld, for, of the two entries made, neither exhibit was considered good enough to secure an award. Mr. T. Statter, who seldom sent anything bad to the shows, owned one of the dogs named the Baron, and, strangely enough, the other exhibit was called Byron, the names evidently in euphony no more far apart, than was the quality of the dogs.

Nottingham in 1872-3 provided classes for smooths, but the Birmingham executive proved very dilatory in encouraging this strain, and it was not until 1874 that Curzon Hall honoured it by giving a special classification for this useful farmer's dog. There is no doubt he is not so handsome as his rough-coated relative; he is equally sagacious and even more useful when in work. North-country farmers say that the heavily-coated dogs cannot do the work on the rough fell lands so well as the smooth, that they are not so hardy and not nearly so fast; and to be successful and thoroughly competent in his duties a collie must have a fair degree of pace.

I have known a smooth dog that could catch an ordinary hare if the latter did not obtain too long a start. I have also seen a rough-coated dog do likewise, but the latter took a short cut up to a gate through which he knew puss would go, and there snapped her, but the smooth dog galloped his game down in a fair course, with points by turns, wrenches, and the ultimate kill. A dangerous sort of dog for the farmer to keep, for in the long run it would be certain to get either its master or some of his servant lads into trouble with the neighbouring gamekeepers. These smooth dogs, crossed with a greyhound, make the best lurchers, and some of the crack rabbit-coursing dogs so commonly used in Lancashire and Durham by the pitmen and others, are so bred. The first cross between the two is re-crossed with the greyhound again and again, until any resemblance to the collie is entirely removed. Such dogs have almost the pace of the pure greyhound, and often enough far more than his skill at the turn or in the kill.

The lowlands of Scotland produce some few smooth-coated collies, which no doubt originally came from this side of the border; their type and character are the same,

Herdwick Herdsman. Herdwick Ewa.

LIBRARY OF
CALIFORNIA

and they are mostly similar in colour. The difficulty in obtaining perfectly smooth-coats in certain strains is great, especially in many of the black and white dogs, which appear to me to approach a variety of their own. The black is almost inclined to be blue, the coat is longer and more open than usual, and there is never the slightest touch of tan or brown appearing—a blue black dog, with more or less white on the neck, chest, and feet. Of such Mr. Alexander Hastie, of Newcastle, has at times shown many splendid representatives, Herdwick Herdsman, Herdwick King, and others to wit. They are all bred in his neighbourhood; for collie character I know nothing to exceed them, and their reputation for work is spoken of equally highly. This ardent admirer of the variety does not, however, stick to colour alone, and awaiting us at the Collie Club's show in London in 1890 was perhaps the very best smooth bitch we ever saw—Herdwick Eva. In type she is perfect; a model collie in size, expression, character, and in all that distinguishes one variety of dog from another. Her ears, too, are small, beautifully carried, and so is her stern; with legs and feet of the best; in colour a dull sable or fawn; and then we come to her defects, one of which was the cause of the judge placing her below, what I considered, comparatively inferior bitches. Her coat is rather too profuse and soft, still a minute examination did not lead one to suspect that her pedigree might include a rough-coated strain. Then she was very much "pig jawed" or "over-shot," a fault or deformity already alluded to. Still, I considered her type so far in advance of that of any other smooth-coated collie I have perhaps ever seen, that I give her a place here, and her portrait faces this page.

Some twenty years or so ago, at the Kendal shows (Westmoreland), some unusually good specimens of the smooth were to be found, one black, tan, and white bitch, the late Mr. Henry Dodd's Fleet, winning time after time, under Mr. W. Lort, who considered her the very best of her variety he ever saw, and all know he is no mean judge. But the best, to my fancy, although some of the judges did not agree with me, was a natural bob-tailed, or tailless bitch, a peculiar brown in colour, shown by Mr. George Fee, and called, I believe, Fan. The expression, character, and form of this bitch were very fine indeed, but being without a tail no doubt handicapped her considerably when in strong competition. Barring in stern, this bitch was an excellent counterpart of Herdwick Eva, alluded to just previously. Both Fleet and Fan belonged to butchers, were used in their trade, and, I believe, Fan was about as good with either cattle or sheep as they can be made. She was something of the form of that good bitch Melody, Mr. W. Arkwright purchased for a good round sum from Mr. T. Marples, but the Kendal bitch was brighter and lighter in colour, had the smaller ears, and was the more sensible in expression.

Of the black, white, and tans, an early and good representative was Mr. W. W. Thomson's (Mitcham) Yarrow, a lowland bitch, I believe, but I never considered her equal to either of the two I have named, and the three were about contemporary. Another excellent specimen of the same colour was Mr. T. B. Swinburne's (Darlington) Lassie, a bitch, I fancy, that won more prizes than any of her variety either before or since, but then she was taken round to all the little shows.

About the same time the brothers, Messrs. J. and T.

Ridley, of Wolsingham, were exhibiting some good dogs at the many shows held in the district, and one of them, a big, strong, sensible-looking bitch, to which I had awarded prizes, became a celebrity in her way and the heroine of a sensational and interesting case in the County Court. This is mentioned here as an instance of the sagacity of the smooth-coated sheep dogs, for the hundreds of stories told, many of which are purely imaginative, are understood to be applicable only to the more fashionable breed with long hair and shaggy jackets.

As it happened, the Messrs. Ridley's bitch was lost from a small show, and, after considerable delay, they sued the secretary for her value, which they estimated at £50. In proof of this they not only gave evidence of her worth as a prize bitch, but, to further enhance her value, Mr. J. Ridley swore that, on one occasion, he, being out on the fells with the same animal, was unfortunate enough to slip and break his leg. He was some miles from his own farm, without any assistance whatever, and of course quite unable to drag himself into any position where he might attract a passing wayfarer, a shepherd, or a farm labourer. Happily, he bethought himself of his dog, and attaching a note to her neck, bid her "Away home, Lassie!" She obeyed the order, the slip of paper on which assistance was asked was noticed, and in due course the friends of the young farmer were guided to the spot, where he was found unable to assist himself. One would have thought so clever a dog as this would have been worth more than the £10 note the County Court judge awarded as damages for its loss. Possibly it saved the man's life.

As to the value of collie dogs, Mr. Montagu Williams, the eminent barrister and distinguished metropolitan police magistrate, in his Memoirs, tells a story of how he found his dog—it was not one of the smooth variety, however,—what it cost him to have it restored, and how, in the end, he contrived to give one of the thieves a *quid pro quo*.

The dog was named Rob, and so great a favourite was he with his master that every precaution was taken to prevent his being stolen at a time when dog thieves were having a good old time—a huge gang of them working together, and exporting all the stolen canines for which they could not obtain a suitable reward. One Sunday morning Rob was missing. Rewards were offered for his recovery, and the police were notified of the theft. Weeks passed by. Then one night a man called to see Mr. Williams, and after beating around the bush somewhat, said " he knew a man who, for £20, would restore the missing favourite." An appointment was made, the barrister promised secrecy, and one cold, wet night Rob was restored to his owner at Bishopsgate-street station, and the £20 paid. The thieves had known the value of the dog in question, had watched the house for days until the opportunity came. Rob was enticed from the door-step, bundled into a cart kept handy for the purpose, and so transferred from the sweets of fashionable West-end to the purlieus of unsavoury Shoreditch.

Two years later Mr. Montagu Williams was called upon to prosecute for dog stealing a man who had frequently been charged and convicted for similar offences, and in the dock was the very fellow who had taken the £20 for restoring the counsel's own dog. The recognition was mutual, but not by any means satisfactory to the prisoner, who grinned a ghastly grin when the learned counsel cast his eye on the fellow he was to prosecute. The case was clear, the thief was convicted of stealing the dog, which at the same time wore a collar, and in the end was found guilty of stealing the collar also. The sentence was eighteen months' imprisonment for the one offence, and twelve months for the other, the two sentences to run consecutively—a terribly severe punishment, which made the dog thief wince, and with an oath declare he had "paid dearly for those pieces."

These stories, at any rate, point a moral or two. If my reader be a dog thief, which may heaven forbid! let him refrain from filching the dog of a popular barrister practising in the criminal courts; and if he own a valuable and sagacious dog, which I hope will be his lot, he will find its merits better appreciated as a companion in a large town than as a faithful servant in a remote country district. I doubt whether Montagu Williams' dog was a handsomer animal than that of Messrs. Ridley; it had not proved so sagacious, still its owner was willing to pay £20 for its return, where a County Court judge refused to give more than £10 damages in the other instance. Whether the dog that got the thief two years and six months' hard labour, which might be likened to a penalty of several hundred pounds, was the better or more valuable of the two, is extremely unlikely.

In addition to the extra good smooth-coated sheep dogs already named are Mr. Swinhoe's Semiramis and Somnus; Mr. Megson's Pickmere and Heatherfield Pearl; and Mr. Mercer's Maida and Drumlin Merl.

The mirled or marbled-colour, with "china" or "wall eyes," as already hinted, is frequently found in the smooth variety, many of the best specimens being of that unusual shade, sometimes intermixed with brown, giving an almost tortoiseshell appearance. It would be interesting to know the reason why the shepherds' dogs, in their varieties, are oftener found with those peculiar eyes than any other breed. Dalmatians are likewise repeatedly seen similarly affected, but terriers less often. A peculiar impression prevails in some localities, that the vision of these "china" eyed dogs is stronger and more powerful than that of others, and that they never contract cataract, ophthalmia, or other diseases of the optics, the truth or otherwise of which I have had no opportunity of determining. These half-white eyes I take to show an approach towards albinoism, and so would be symbolical of weakness rather than of strength. Mr. Howard Mapplebeck's Fan was a bitch of this mirled or tortoiseshell colour, and Dr. James, Mr. E. Hutton, Mr. G. Hall, Mr. Megson, Mr. S. Boddington, and others have likewise introduced good specimens with the china eyes, which, as a rule, have not been of their own breeding.

Useful animal as is the smooth collie, he has quite failed to become popular, the reason for which is not far to seek. He lacks beauty, and is not interesting in appearance. The story told on another page is proof of his intelligence; he is easier to find of fair quality than his more popular relative, and when found does not cost nearly so much money. Ten pounds is a good round price to give for a smooth collie, and instances of a hundred pounds being paid for a rough dog are commoner than are cases of twenty pounds given for the other, which, after all, carries less dirt into the house, and so is more fitted for a drawing room companion. He might be made fashionable yet, were society to take him in hand, and I am confident that as a dog he would rise to the occasion and demean himself with true aristocratic *hauteur*. Let some enterprising admirer make an attempt to breed him to colour, for bright orange or red with the snowy circle round his neck, a white breast and a tip of white at the end of his brush, no dog would look handsomer. As he is, his less bright colours are not sufficiently attractive to the eye, and modern fancy just now runs in a craze for gaudiness. Nor have poets sung of his merits, nor distinguished painters immortalised him on their canvases.

## CHAPTER V.

The Old English "Bob-tailed" Sheep Dog—His Origin—Reinagle's Illustration in the "Sportsman's Cabinet"—Richardson's Description—"Idstone"—Early Classes—Dr. Edwardes-Ker's Opinion—Description and Standard of Points.

THERE appears to be considerable difference of opinion as to the reputation the old-fashioned, bob-tailed, rough-coated English sheep or drover's dog ought to bear. His admirers praise his docility and intelligence, and rave about the beauty of "his bright blue eyes," and the rugged luxury of his hairy jacket. His detractors say he is a fraud and a deception, ugly to the mind educated to beauty, and by no means either so docile and intelligent as a guardian of the flocks and herds should be. As a fact, the Collie Club refuses altogether to acknowledge him, so he is left to the tender mercies of a few enthusiastic admirers who formed a special club of their own to promote and foster their fancy, and it will be the fault of the public rather than of themselves if the bob-tailed sheep dog does not blossom into a fashionable beauty. He is certainly a handsomer animal than the British bulldog, but for elegance of shape and adaptability as a

## No Connection with Wales. 81

household pet, he cannot compare with the modern collie and the fox terrier.

How this old-fashioned variety came about history affords no record. My idea as to how he was brought into the world without a tail, or at any rate with but a very short one, is given in a preceding chapter, in which it will be seen I hold an opinion different from Dr. Edwardes-Ker, whose remarks on the subject follow in due course, and will no doubt be read with interest, and valued as coming from one of our foremost and most accomplished admirers of the variety.

Many counties have laid claim to the paternity of the bobtailed sheep dog, either through local admirers, or by writers on canine matters. Wales has been said to possess the most right to the breed, because Mr. R. J. Lloyd Price, of Rhiwlas, near Bala, has occasionally kept a few specimens, and because his grandfather had likewise been an admirer of their rough beauty. As a fact, the sort of sheep dog indigenous to the Principality, if it has an indigenous strain at all, is a little mirled, or blue-grey and white, or tortoiseshell, smooth-coated dog, with china or wall eyes. The bob-tails of Mr. Edward Lloyd (Mr. Price's grandfather), originally came from the Southdowns, and so had no hereditary connection with Wales at all.

Then, running away northwards, Scotland has laid claim to their original possession, and in some districts the strain survives in the "bearded sheep dog," which, however, has not a "bob-tail." Classes for this variety are occasionally met with at the local shows. I believe that the old English sheep dog was at one time pretty equally distributed through various parts of the kingdom, and of late years has been most numerous in those localities where a dog of his description was required. He has been found most

G

useful as a drover's dog—therefore, as such he is oftimes found, and I have seen a greater number of these rough "bob-tails" following the cattle men through the streets of London than in any other locality. An extra good specimen may, under such circumstances, be at times met with and picked up from these men for a "crown and a pot of four half." "Idstone," alluding to the fact that on the Wiltshire downs these dogs were, when he wrote about twenty years ago, repeatedly bought and sold for a few shillings, and at the large fairs it was the usual thing for these dogs to change hands; the new owner having the dog handed over to him, with "a collar twisted out of a green hazel and a few feet of old cord." Bewick's "bob-tailed" collie is smooth-coated, of any of the prevailing colours; but, like all engravings of this master of his craft, his "cur-dog" is a most characteristic example of what the animal was at that day.

Few of the old writers refer to the breed. In the "Sportsman's Cabinet" (1803-4), an excellent illustration is given by Reinagle, the dog being just such a one as would be met with at the present day, were he favoured by a pleasanter and less villainous expression, which is given him, perhaps unintentionally, by his two peculiarly yellow coloured eyes. It is still held that the eyes should be light in colour, not yellow, but of a pale blue approaching white, "wall" or "china" eyes indeed, which I have heard named "pearl." Unfortunately, the literary description in the "Cabinet" does not in any way apply to the illustration, and so one has to turn elsewhere in search of special information on the subject: Nor does there appear to be anything more interesting to be gleaned from contemporary writers, who appear to have treated all varieties of the sheep dog as pretty much the same, it being quite the exception to make even a little difference between those of the highlands and those of the lowlands.

Approaching our own time, Youatt (1845) gives us a drawing of an English sheep dog, which is an ordinary grey and white or black and white Scotch collie without a tail on, or with but a meagre stump of the caudal appendage. This author tells us little or nothing about him beyond suggesting that, in the more enclosed districts, where strength is often needed to turn an obstinate sheep, the English sheep dog is crossed with some larger dog, as the rough terrier, sometimes the pointer, or now and then with the bull dog, and thus, he says, are obtained the larger sheep dog or drovers' dogs. One wonders if the scientific Youatt ever saw even a single instance of any of these crosses, and where he would have obtained his rough terrier stronger than an ordinary sheep dog? Still, such statements are handed down as history, to be believed no doubt by many persons who have no knowledge to the contrary. The bob-tailed sheep dog was never manufactured in that way.

Richardson (1850), who evidently knows more of this dog than the more popular author Youatt, alludes to "the shepherd's dog or collie, and the shepherd's dog of England;" and says the latter is "the larger, the stronger, and has much the appearance of a cross with the great rough water dog. It is coarser in the muzzle and coat, and is destitute of tail. In sagacity, I believe it to be fully equal to its more northern relative. About London, and in many parts of England, the drover's dog, which is chiefly used in driving sheep, is without any tail. This, however, is not the natural form of the animal, for the tail is destroyed when very young, not by cutting off, but by extracting the bone, an inhuman practice technically called 'stringing,' generally performed by pulling out that part with the teeth. After this, the fleshy part of the tail contracts to a mere tubercle, and is wholly concealed among the shaggy hair of the animal. Dogs treated in this manner are said to endure much more exertion with less fatigue than those in which the tail is entire; and whether this be the fact or not, the degree of fatigue these dogs can undergo is truly astonishing. Nor is their sagacity less wonderful, for they can divide the drove into any sections that may be required, drive one section one way and another another way, whatever may be the number; and after the sections are once parcelled off to purchasers, they can bring back again with the most unerring certainty any individual which has left its sections, and joined another. These offices are generally performed by barking and by manœuvring alone, without touching the sheep with the mouth; or, if that operation be necessary, the dogs merely lay hold of the sheep, and force them into the intended direction by holding the wool, without biting the skin, or even separating that portion of the wool by which they take hold."

Here is a character which may be born by any other variety of sheep dog, and "stringing" the puppy to give it strength is merely a vulgar opinion, which obtains in ignorant circles equally to the terrier and the spaniel. "Aye," said a fellow to me one day, "your terriers are always rare strong-backed 'uns, because you cut their tails properly." I did it for fancy, not to strengthen the dog in any particular, which it certainly does not. Other writers have said that the "bob-tailed" sheep dog will run over the backs of a flock of sheep huddled together in order to head them, a feat equally often (possibly oftener) performed by the ordinary collie.

Our old friend "Idstone" appears to have had a special knack of noticing these drovers' dogs, they were common in his Dorsetshire district; he often alludes to them in his articles, and the opinions I had formed of the disposition of the variety, that charming and practical writer actually corroborates. I found the rough old English "bob-tails" more or less surly in disposition, slow and methodical in their movements, with a peculiar love of home and their old masters, and such as I have been acquainted with have invariably been very loth to make friends with strangers, or even with their new owners, until they became well acquainted with them. As a rule, any other variety kindly spoken to and fed, will take to a new master in a day or two, and, so long as an opportunity is not negligently afforded, will not endeavour to escape. On the contrary, the "bob-tail" is very slow to make new friends, and a week, or even a fortnight or longer, elapses before he will settle comfortably down in a new home.

A peculiarity these dogs possess is found in the manner they express their pleasure. There is an old saw to the effect that it would be more wonderful if the tail wagged the dog rather than the dog wagged his tail. In the "bob-tail" you have pretty nearly the extraordinary part of the saying, for, though the dog has no tail, or at any rate a very diminutive one, to wag, he must wag something to show his delight, so he waggles his hindquarters and body in a very funny, and at the same time in a most peculiar, manner. It is said, with a minimum amount of truth, that, by this habit one can tell whether the short tail is natural or whether it has been made so artificially!

Returning to the disposition of the animal, "Idstone" says the English sheep dog is slower and heavier than the collie. I must add that he is not so sprightly as his northern cousin, nor on the whole so sagacious. He partakes, as do all the dogs (especially pastoral ones) of the character of his teacher. The English shepherd is surly, silent, and for the most part ignorant, and he has an especial dislike to strangers. Then this writer argues that the dog takes after his master. But this evil character for the English shepherd is by no means correct, only in a slight degree so as applied to those of the southern and midland counties, and not at all to the northern ones, who, had "Idstone" been acquainted with them, would no doubt have been coupled with the Scotch caretakers of sheep.

The same writer calls these dogs "blue-grizzled, rough-haired, large-limbed, surly, small-eared and small-eyed, leggy, bob-tailed dogs," and says they are chiefly found in Oxfordshire, Wiltshire, Berkshire, Hants, and Dorsetshire. He continues, they "would obey no lighter instrument of punishment than an iron-shod crook, listen to no voice unless seasoned with a strong provincial twang, and coil himself up on none other than the inevitable drab blanket coat into whose sleeves no shepherd was ever known to put his arms."

I think from these statements the conclusion may safely be reached that at present, and for some time back, these "old English bob-tails" are, and have been, for the most part confined to the southern counties, where the level roads and comparatively easy country to work are much more fitted for their somewhat ponderous frames than are the rough hills and steep mountains of Wales and other portions of the British Isles. That the animal best adapted for the use of the locality in which it is found and preserved, is applicable equally to dogs as to cattle, sheep, and horses; and so the lumbersome old English bob-tailed sheep dog is not indigenous either on the Welsh mountains or to the Scottish moorlands; he is of the southerns southernly, and no doubt performs the duties well for which he is kept by his admirers.

Quite recently, at the close of 1889, Mr. Freeman Lloyd, a great admirer of the breed, contributed some articles thereon to *Turf, Field, and Farm*, published in America, the series being subsequently reprinted in pamphlet form. This writer claims rather too much for his favourite, for he says he is faster than the collie, and "can run round any dog with the exception of greyhounds and deerhounds." This remark must of course be taken *cum grano salis*; but some of Mr. Lloyd's observations are interesting, especially where he alludes to the bark of the bob-tail, which he says is so peculiar that he can "recognise one a quarter of a mile off, or if in a show a dog sets barking, I know at once whether it is the voice of a 'bob-tail' or not. It is a sharp ringing voice, something like that of a collie's, but with more volume or power." This writer's description is much the same as my own and Dr. Ker's, excepting that he deals very leniently with soft, curly coats, and is not a great stickler for colours. The three illustrations he gives—viz., Mrs. Mayhew's Gwen; Sir Guy, and an American dog called Bob—are all distinct in type, the latter very much so, and an extremely moderate specimen. He, however, recommends the coat of the Sir Cavendish type as the best, and the short, hard coat he has no sympathy with. Mr Lloyd speaks highly of the intelligence of this variety, and, like all enthusiasts, rather overstates his case.

I do not consider the "bob-tail" a great success as a show dog. Birmingham has the credit of giving him the first class in which he was able to compete against dogs only of his own variety, and, as a rule, when such an opportunity is afforded, one may conclude that the future of the dog so honoured is more or less assured. Will it be so in this instance? for, this early class was provided so far back as 1873, when there were only three entries. There were but thirteen entries in 1889, although the formation of the club the year before, and the commencement of an attempt to popularise them, resulted in an excellent collection of twenty in the two classes at Curzon Hall, a number which has not been reached at any show since that time, nor had this record been approached earlier. In 1873 the three entries were a poor sample—so indifferent in fact that only a second prize was awarded. Two years later Mr. Lloyd Price won with a good-looking dog called Bob, and since then, as a rule, all the prizes have been given. Other exhibitions of the kind that have provided these distinct classes have received no greater support, though with ever varying fashion, one cannot divine the result that might be brought about in two or three years' time. Personally, I do not believe that this variety of dog is destined to obtain any great hold on our human affections. His disposition is at present not quite suitable for a domestic companion, though improved associations might remedy this, and his long shaggy coat (especially the abundance of hair on his legs) must, for reasons of cleanliness, make him unfitted as an inhabitant of the drawing-room, which, popularised as the club wishes him to be, would be his place.

## Dr. Edwardes-Ker's Opinion.

Here is what Dr. Ker writes:

"Many hundred years ago, when our island was principally primeval forest, with but few clearings, it must necessarily have been infested with wolves, bears, and the lesser British carnivoræ, and to protect the flocks and herds it must have been requisite to have a large and powerful dog, able to cope with such formidable and destructive foes, able to undergo any amount of fatigue, and with a jacket to withstand all vicissitudes of weather, for his avocation was an everyday one; day and night, and in all weathers, was he watching and battling with heat and storm and marauding foes. What other dog but the old English sheep-dog possesses attributes necessary for the multifarious duties urged upon such a business?

"There we find the sagacity, the activity, the enduring strength, the dauntless courage, and the weatherproof jacket combined to such a degree in no other British dog. His origin is lost in the dim obscurity of buried centuries. To my mind his antiquity and concentration of purity of strain are fully shown in the fact, that if there be a strain of old English sheep-dog blood many generations back in any breed of dog, you may stake your life that a typical specimen will every now and again show itself in the litter produced by utterly dissimilar breeds, no matter whether it be a retriever, lurcher, spaniel, or cur of low degree. I have known it occur in many instances, and have owned first-class sheep-dogs whose parentage would make one's hair stand on end with amazement at the fearful incongruity of its component parts. Apparently not one drop of sheep-dog blood for generations, and yet there is the unmistakable youngster—

sometimes tailless, more often with a three-inch stump—brought into the world jet-black, with his characteristic white markings, and in a few weeks, chameleon-like, he gradually assumes the silvery-lilac livery of his ancient British ancestors, and makes his bow to the public as a pigeon-blue and white English sheep-dog, 'breeder and pedigree unknown.'

"Does not all this point to his ancient purity, this powerful concentration of sanguinity which is irrepressible? One sees many theories put forward with regard to his tailless heritage, but I am convinced that, originally nothing but a sport, this peculiarity has been carefully selected by shepherds and stockmen who preferably bred from a naturally tailless strain, to save themselves the trouble of docking their dogs, and so rendering them exempt from the penalties of the Forest Laws.

"With regard to the sagacity of this breed I consider it has few equals, and certainly no superior. In a large dairy farm I know of, there is a dog which will fetch up individual cows as they are required to be milked, distinguishing those which he has already fetched up, and after being milked are allowed to mix with the rest of the herd. When quite a lad I remember seeing an old grizzle and white sheep dog lying outside a farmhouse here in Suffolk, which three weeks or a month before was purchased in Dumfries; he worked a herd of bullocks all the way from his Scottish home to the eastern corner of Suffolk by road. After remaining comfortably for a fortnight in his new quarters, one day he was missing, and no tidings could be gleaned of him in the neighbourhood; and no wonder, for within the week his Suffolk purchaser received a letter informing him the old dog was safe back in Dumfries. This incident occurred to-

## Size of the "Bob-Tail."

Mr. Edmund Tye, of The Moat Farm, Dallinghoo, Suffolk, who was my informant.

"With regard to the size of the original breed, I cannot help thinking he was a much larger dog than is seen nowadays. They have a dwarfed appearance; they are all 'little big'uns,' and to obtain that characteristic there must have been the size sometime or other. And I confess I prefer the big ones, they have a grander appearance, a big blue and white dog of twenty-five inches catches the eye, and he can carry a heavy coat without looking like a smothered Yorkshire terrier or a door-mat-like Isle of Skye. Shepherds prefer the little ones, why? because they do not eat so much, and can dodge in and out of the furze bushes after rabbits. These men do not want sheep-dogs nowadays, they prefer whippets. The well-known dog, Sir Guy, who in his day was almost invincible on the show-bench, was once sold for two shillings because he fell head over heels over a rabbit: and to my idea that old dog, when in full coat, was the grandest sheep-dog in existence. Look at his mighty frame, active as a kitten; his massive head with the truncated muzzle so rarely seen, the tiny ears, the hard coat, and, above all things, the utter absence of 'poodleness.' The fashion in bob-tailed sheep-dogs is becoming poodle-like! but it is very, very wrong.

"I admire a heavy coat on the show-bench, for there ought to be a superabundance of jacket to allow for wear and tear in the bushes when at work, but let us carefully avoid anything that approaches the curliness of the poodle. A beautiful and picturesque dog was Mr. Wilke's Watchman; but he was not a sheep-dog, his coat was in ringlets, and his ears 'as big as a blacksmith's apron.' Steer clear of big ears and curly coats, but do not go to the contrary extreme, and get an absolutely straight coat. An old English sheep-dog's coat should be shaggy, and all I can liken it to, is to that peculiar style of growth of hair frequently seen on a clodhopping countryman's head—in a word, shock-headed: one lock growing this way, and another that way; no curl, but a sort of head you could wipe your boots on!

"Suffolk has produced most of the best show specimens of late years—to wit, Sir Guy, Sir Lucifer, Sir Lancelot, Mayor of Newport, Blue Ruin, Welsh Sensation, Welsh Marvel, Dame Dorothy, the American Dame Judith. Dame Margery, bought in Norwich Market sixteen years ago, for half-a-crown, was the dam of the last Olympia Cup Winner, Sir Caradoc, and grand-dam of Sir Cavendish. Nellie II. is another sterling good bitch, great in size and style, a trifle soft in coat, but there is no poodle resemblance; her sire and dam were sheep-dogs of the type beloved by drovers, long and strong, and rough in body and mind. No doubt the best bitch of the variety we have at present is Mrs. Mayhew's Gwen, a grey or blue and white, with a correct coat, which is, however, somewhat spoiled by being over-groomed for show-bench purposes. She has won a great number of prizes at most of our leading shows. For colour I prefer the pigeon-blue, not washed out, but well defined, standing out clearly against nice white markings, and, if possible, a wall-eye or two; but any shade of grizzle is equally correct. Sables and brindles and blacks are an abomination! Dogs twenty-four or twenty-five inches, or larger if possible. Bitches as big as one can get them, both sexes being strong and masculine in appearance, with length and strength, well knit, but

Sir Cavendish.

not cloddy like guinea pigs ; at the same time size should not weigh against type and quality. The more *hair* on the jaws the better; I mean hair, too, not wool.

"I remember, as quite a boy, that the generality of old English sheep-dogs were grey or blue in colour, with white feet, and white head and neck. Nearly every drover had one, and every shepherd, for we had no collies then. An old drover who died here (near Woodbridge) last year at a very great age, named Chuffy Plant, told me that my dogs were the right stamp, but they were 'little rat-dawg things'; too much quality; were not big enough or strong enough. I could not argue with the old man, as I felt he was an authority, but I explained to him that I had to breed for the show-bench. Whereupon he anathematised the show-bench with this remark: 'Drat it all, ye can allus breed minnifers; dround them and rear the big'uns!' Minnifer or miniver signifies the weasel, but is a term applied in Suffolk to any small or weedy specimen of animals."

Sir Cavendish, the dog so admirably drawn on the adjoining page, I consider the handsomest and best of his breed hitherto seen; moreover, he possesses to a remarkable degree all the attributes required to approach perfection. He may well be considered the typical specimen of his variety, and, as such, particular trouble has been taken to obtain his full description, which, in combination with the general one already given, will enable those interested to know exactly the sort of animal required in this variety.

Sir Cavendish is a pigeon-blue and white dog, with correct markings, 23½ in. in height at the shoulder, 52lb. in weight, with very small flat ears, almost entirely buried in coat, which is long, thick, and shaggy, free from either straightness or curl. It is 11 in. long upon his loins and hind-quarter, whilst his face and legs are evenly and equally clothed with hair, the front of the legs carrying as much coat as the back part of the same. His tail is a very short, natural stump, and when he "wags" it, he does so vertically, not horizontally, which his owner says is a peculiarity he has looked for in vain in any other strain. His sire, Sir Caradoc, is well known as a very large pigeon-blue and white dog, rather soft in coat, but showing remarkable character; these two inheriting their beautiful colour and sheep-dog characteristics from old Dame Margery, who was also a "natural bob." Her strain is remarkable for possessing double dewclaws upon one or both hind legs. Dame Ruth, the dam of the subject of our illustration, was a small bitch of great character, by Jockey, half-brother to Sir Guy out of Bess, by Sir Guy out of Dame Margery; and it is interesting to know that, although Sir Guy has never sired anything up to bench form, still there is a concentration of his blood in very many of our best specimens.

One other interesting fact remains to be told with regard to the way their breeder, Dr. Ker, hit off the pigeon-blue colour. He had been breeding blue grizzle with blue grizzle for several years, hoping to produce the coveted pigeon-blue, but to his chagrin the puppies came darker with each succeeding generation, and smaller likewise. The thought then struck him of Jockey to get the size back—never dreaming about colour. Jockey was then mated to Dame Margery, and she bred two dog puppies at fourteen years old. One of these was of the long-coveted colour—he became Sir Caradoc; whilst the other was nearly white, with blue ears and a tan cheek.

Jockey was a smooth dog, with a wonderfully thick, short, weatherproof jacket, like long plush, and was a yellow sable. Now, who would ever have thought of producing pigeon-blue from such an incongruity? Even now Dr. Ker says he despairs of maintaining this lovely hue, as all his puppies are born black or sable; now and again one of the blacks turning blue when about six months old. Sir Cavendish was jet black as a whelp, so was Dame Leah. Dame Judith was a lovely blue-blotting paper colour at six months; but as a whelp she was of that peculiar rusty-black colour only to be seen in the tall hat of an undertaker, or of a superannuated post-lad. She was sired by that undefeated champion, Sir Guy, out of the dark blue-mirl, Dame Dorothy.

Sir Guy's grandsire was a short-coated, mouse-coloured dog, in fact, a dun, bred by a Mr. Brinkley, somewhere down on the Sudbourne Marshes, and his grand-dam was a bitch of the same colour belonging to Shepherd Mills of Eyke. Very large dogs these were—much bigger than anything of the present day, in fact, Sir Guy's sire, Mill's Bob, would make almost two of him with regard to size and general massiveness. He could catch a hare, so it was not all lumber; he was 25½ in. at the shoulder, on very short legs, was a natural bob-tail, of a peculiar grizzled-dun colour, with very small rose ears. He died in the Fernyhurst Kennels at a great age, and to the last was more than a match for any dog his size; in fact, old Mills gave him away because he had killed so many dogs in his neighbourhood. So much for Bob, a comparatively smooth dog, with a more weatherproof jacket than half the overcoated winners on the show bench to-day.

The following are the points to be allowed in judging the Old English sheep dog:

| | |
|---|---|
| Shape of head and colour of eyes (the latter preferred pearl, light blue, or china) | 20 |
| Teeth | 5 |
| Ears | 10 |
| Neck and shoulders | 5 |
| Legs and feet | 10 |
| Back, loins, and hind-quarters | 10 |
| Coat | 20 |
| Colour (any shade of blue, grizzled, or mirled, with or without white markings) | 10 |
| Size (weight from 45lb. to 60lb.) | 10 |
| | 100 |

Disqualifications: soft, curly, poodle-like coat, black and tan and brindled colours.

From time to time good "bob-tails" have been shown by Mr. R. Abbott, Hingham, Norfolk; by Mr. W. G. Weager, Streatham, Surrey; by Mr. Morton Campbell, Brechin, N.B.; by Mr. D. Parry Thomas, Pontypridd, whose Mayor of Cardiff was a great favourite in the show ring; by Mr. Freeman Lloyd, London; Mr. E. T. Rees, Cardiff, and by Mr. R. J. Lloyd Price, already alluded to, whose Belle of Ranelagh was good enough to win at Birmingham and elsewhere.

The special club to promote the interests of the old-fashioned English bob-tailed sheep dog was established in 1888, and, not to be behind similar institutions, forthwith compiled a list of rules, and submitted the following description of the dog as he ought to be, with the scale of points by which he is to be judged. How far they coincide with what Dr. Ker has contributed, and what I have written, will, no doubt, be observed by those who trouble themselves to peruse this chapter. As I have hinted, Sir Cavendish is acknowledged by all whose opinions are worthy of consideration to be about the best specimen we have, and he must be taken as our model.

The description and points of the "Old English sheep dog," as adopted by the club, of which Mr. P. W. Knight, 14, Blenheim-road, London, N.W., is the secretary, are as follows :

*Skull.*—Capacious and rather squarely formed, giving plenty of room for brain power. The parts over the eyes should be well arched, and the whole well covered with hair as defined in "coat."

*Jaw.*—Should be fairly long and square. The "stop' should be defined, but not to a great extent.

*Eyes.*—These, of course, vary in different colours of dogs. In the dark blue shades they should be dark brown. In the lighter colours they will be found to follow them, and become paler in shade, while where white predominates a wall or marble eye may be considered very typical.

*Nose.*—Always black in colour, fairly large and capacious.

*Teeth.*—Strong and firm, and should be evenly placed in the jaw. Working dogs often have their incisors broken off. This is in no way detrimental.

*Ears.*—Medium sized and carried close to the head, coated with hair of a moderate length.

*Legs.*—The fore legs should be straight and possess plenty of bone. They should remove the body a medium height off the ground, without approaching legginess. They should be well-coated all round.

*Feet.*—Moderately large; round ; toes well arched and pads capacious and hard.

*Tail.*—This is a most important point in the Old English sheep dog. Without a doubt many dogs are bred without the slightest approach to a caudal appendage, while on the other hand, some in the litters will be found with half, three-quarters, and whole length tails. The breeding of those without tails should be encouraged and persevered with, and be given preference to in judging, providing the dogs are good elsewhere. A tail of any length takes away the appearance and the corkiness of the dog. A docked dog can generally be detected by the bluntness at the end of stump.

*Neck and Shoulders.*—The neck should be fairly long, arched and graceful, and well coated with hair. The shoulders should be set on slopingly, and the dog generally be found to stand lower at the shoulders than on his hind quarters.

*Body.*—Rather short and very compact. The ribs should be well sprung, and brisket deep and capacious. The loin should be very stout, and to a certain extent arched, while the hind quarters should be bulky, and the hams densely covered with coat, very often of a softer and more woolly description than is to be found on other parts of the body.

*Coat.*—Profuse and of good texture, *i.e.*, fairly hard and strong. There should also be a double or under coat.

*Colour.*—Varies, but preference should be given to dark blue, light or pigeon blue and steel grey dogs. The colours are generally intermixed with white, which imparts to the dog a more attractive appearance. White collars, legs, chest and face should be encouraged.

*Height.*—Fair stand and measurement of the shoulder from 20 inches upwards. The bitches, of course, smaller than the dogs. Great height is not to be encouraged, for it takes away the corkiness and cobbiness of the dog.

*General Appearance.*—He is a strong, compact looking dog, profusely coated all over. He generally gallops with his head down, having a peculiar springing style of movement, and his whole make and shape of body should strike one as being very much after the style of a bear. An animal which people, not conversant with the breed, will generally quote as an analogy.

SCALE OF POINTS.

| | |
|---|---|
| Skull | 10 |
| Jaw | 5 |
| Eyes | 5 |
| Nose | 5 |
| Colour | 10 |
| Teeth | 5 |
| Ears | 5 |
| Legs (if coated) | 10 |
| Tail (undocked) | 10 |
| Neck and shoulders | 10 |
| Body, loin, hind-quarters | 10 |
| Coat | 10 |
| Marking | 5 |
| | 100 |

The above description has not been received with any great degree of favour in some quarters, still I consider it together with the scale of points, worth printing here. At any rate, they give some amount of completeness to what has been written on the subject. Without going into any minute criticisms of the matter the club has put together, I may take exception to what is said about the feet being moderately large, and also their particulars as to the tail. Personally I believe a skilful operator can reduce the stern of a puppy in such a manner as to make it an absolute impossibility for even an expert to tell whether this shortening be natural or otherwise. And we must not forget that natural "bob-tails" are rarer than the artificial ones, and that in the same litter puppies with tails of varying length or shortness are produced.

## CHAPTER VI.

TRIALS WITH SHEEP — THE FIRST MEETING — CHIEF GATHERINGS — NORTH OF ENGLAND AND WALES — THE QUEEN PRESENT — A TYPICAL TRIAL — DESCRIPTION OF THE COMPETING DOGS — RULES, REGULATIONS, AND GENERAL MANAGEMENT.

SINCE the trials of shepherds' dogs were instituted at Bala, in Wales, by Mr. R. J. Lloyd Price, of Rhiwlas, Mr. F. Parmeter, and Mr. T. Ellis, in 1873, similar meetings have become fairly popular in other parts of the country—that they have not become more so causes some little astonishment. The British public is usually ready to patronise any sport or amusement that bears any interesting feature, especially where animals are concerned. As a means of observing the intelligence of the dog, these collie trials have no equal. The sagacity of the shepherd's companion can thereby be tested to its utmost, without in the slightest degree putting the dog to any unusual exertion, or distressing it or the sheep which are used for the purpose. On a fine day no more interesting sight need be desired than to see a number of highly-trained shepherds' dogs one after another driving and working a little flock of sheep in an almost perfect manner. The country air is fresh and healthy on the hillsides, all the surroundings of the gathering are thoroughly rural and invigorating, and the good humour and friendliness of the owners of the competitors towards each other, appear in marked contrast to the jealousies so often present at sporting meetings of other kinds. Then, too, the farmer and shepherd enjoy the sociability; and the silver cup or money prize, which may be offered by their landlord, is always an object of attainment that takes higher rank almost than the piece of plate won at the local agricultural show, held in the autumn, for the best cow or horse, or the most valued pen of sheep in the district.

In these times of peculiar changes no stone should be left unturned that is likely to sustain the good feeling not always prevailing between landowner and tenant. That which is good for the one is equally good for the other, and in two or three localities with which I am acquainted where such competitions as collie trials are held, and in a great measure supported by the landed interest, the friendliness and good understanding between the two classes cannot be surpassed; rents are paid with promptitude, and agriculture flourishes amain. Without going quite so far as to suggest such competitive trials as a panacea for political unpleasantness and agricultural depression, there is no doubt these meetings and district agricultural societies bring the land occupier and the land owner into touch with each other, provocative of friendliness that can scarcely be secured by any other means.

Personally, I should delight to see almost every agricultural county in England with its association of this kind. Such would, in all likelihood, enhance the value of the collie dog in its proper role, and so far allow the farmer to have another iron in the fire likely to assist him in replenishing well-nigh exhausted coffers after a bad season, besides giving to the well-trained guardian of his flocks, at any rate, a value quite equal to that realised by a similar animal whose only recommendation lies in its handsome face and showily shaggy jacket.

The earliest trials of dogs with sheep took place in Wales, and have been continued in the principality ever since, where, perhaps, they enjoy greater popularity than elsewhere. Similar meetings are held in the north of England, and for eleven years great gatherings have taken place in various localities in the counties of Westmoreland, Cumberland, Lancashire, and Yorkshire, under the auspices of the North-Western Counties Sheep Dog Trials Association, established in 1878. Mr. F. Punchard, Kirkby Lonsdale, is the secretary, and Lady Bective has proved a great supporter of the association, on most occasions personally presenting the prizes. The principal Welsh meeting is that of the Llangollen sheep dog trials, of which Her Majesty the Queen is gracious patroness, and Captain Best, Vivod, Llangollen, the secretary and moving spirit. To the latter in a great measure is due the success this meeting has attained.

Last year, in 1889, on the visit of Her Majesty to Wales, Capt. Best had the honour of arranging sundry trials in which the best dogs in the Principality and from Lancashire were brought to show their skill in presence of the Royal party. Some excellent displays resulted; Her Majesty expressed great gratification with the work performed, and was pleased to compliment the shepherds on the possession of such sagacious collies, a variety of dog of which, as stated earlier on, the Queen is a great admirer. Other gatherings are held at times in various parts of the country, sometimes in connection with the Dublin Dog Show, and once at the Alexandra Palace in 1876, under the auspices of the Kennel Club. This was, however, not altogether successful, and a chance was thus lost that might have led to such meetings being made annual. The only dog that did really good work here was Mr. J. Thomas' red bitch Madie who won the champion cup against all comers, including several from North of England as well as from Wales. The representatives of the latter, however, took all the honours. Colonel le Gendre Starkie and Mr. John Williams were the judges. But Wales and the North of England are the centres from which collie trials spring, owing, no doubt, to the facilities the shepherds on the hills possess of bringing their dogs to a state of perfection. The wild, active, diminutive Welsh sheep are excellent material upon which to train the dogs, and equally good in this respect are the black faces and Herdwicks of the English Lake district.

The big, heavy sheep of the Sussex Downs, the Lincolnshire Wolds, and the Shropshire Pastures require little driving or looking after. Kept in inclosed land, they have not the opportunities afforded them of straying, such as fall to the lot of their more plebeian cousins, who find their living on the extensive commons and vast moorlands quite necessary for the existence and proper preservation of those mountain sheep which give us such excellent mutton. Yet it is always possible to send a good flock of the proper sort of sheep into any county, an example of which Mr. Price set at the Alexandra Palace trials, already alluded to, when one of his shepherds brought about a hundred all the distance from Rhiwlas by rail and road, and they stood the two hundred and thirty mile journey very well.

The earliest gathering ever held appears to have been most successful and pleasant in every particular. There was a good entry, including competitors from various parts of the country, and the novelty of the thing and the excellent work done by the shepherds' dogs appear to have pleased the visitors immensely. May be it would be well here to mention the winner of chief honours. This was Mr. James Thompson's Tweed, and the names of both the owner and his dog convey their nationality. Tweed was so good looking an animal that, after securing the competition, he was awarded the special prize as the handsomest sheep dog on the ground. The *Field* reporter at that time speaks in high terms of Sam, a Northumberland dog "of the Ridley stock," whose performances were excellent, but he did not appear to be quite so well handled as the winner, and Sam came but third. The general arrangements here at this first meeting appear to have been very similar to those continued since by the North-Western Trials Association, and by others held at Oswestry, Llanberis, Silecroft, and elsewhere.

These arrangements are simplicity itself, and with two or three good managers undertaking the work in hand, the cost of the preliminaries is not great. In the first instance, suitable ground is to be found. Of necessity this need not be in one field, but must be of an extent —of say, extending in one direction about half to three-quarters of a mile by about a quarter of a mile in breadth. From a note made by me at the time, I find that at the trials held at Gilsland, near Carlisle, in 1885 the dogs had to drive their sheep something over 800 yards, and the trial ground covered about 90 acres. The latter, of course, not including the portions occupied by the spectators. Here, on our wild, bleak fells of Cumberland the space to be obtained was almost unlimited. As circumstances occur, these estimates may be extended or decreased at will. Having secured such suitable ground, the next thing is to draw out a plan denoting the course over which the dogs have to drive their sheep, the positions where the worker of the dog, the judges, and officials are to stand, the location of the spectators, and the place where the pen is erected into which the competitors have to drive their flock.

The course is indicated by a succession of flags placed at intervals, on the far side of which the dogs drive the

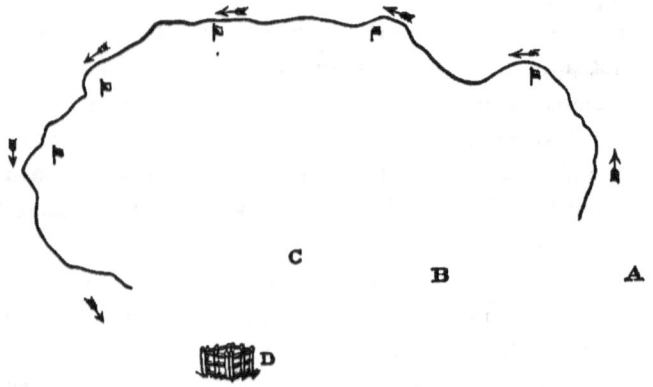

sheep, the time occupied and the manner in which the work is done being placed to the credit or otherwise of the competitors. The above sketch will assist to convey an idea as to a plan of the ground.

The sheep are liberated near A, the shepherd standing at B sends his dog to the sheep, which are to be driven in the direction indicated by the arrows on the far side of the flags to D, a pen of hurdles into which the sheep have to be driven. The judges and officials stand at C, a position from which they can observe all the work.

This trial ground should not be level like a racecourse; it is better more or less undulating; with a footpath or two running across; a dry burn or ghyll to pass over; a gap or opening in a hedge or fence to be driven through. Roughish land is best of all, even if it lay along a hill side, a commencement of the task being to drive the sheep up the incline, and away from the shepherd. Then along the outside or far side of the flags to the boundary flag, which must be properly rounded, and so on the far side of other flags on the return journey, to three hurdles forming a pen, with the fourth hurdle away, leaving an opening. Through the latter the little flock has to be sent, the worker of the dog being allowed to assist as he likes, without, however, touching the sheep. Until now the shepherd has worked his collie from the spot where it was originally let loose, and sent to find the sheep which had been separated from a flock inclosed and out of sight. Were the whole of the sheep in view of those to be driven the latter would make back to them, and totally refuse to be taken as intended.

As to the sheep : These ought to be either of the Welsh breed, the black or of some grey-faced Scotch variety, or Herdwicks, taken from various flocks. Each dog drives three different sheep, two being from one farm, and the third from another. This arrangement makes the task more difficult, the sheep not knowing each other, and when one breaks away considerable skill is required to get it to its companions again. Sometimes the latter cannot be done, so the worker of the dog by whistling, calling, or by movements of the arms, lets his favourite know that the two must be driven to the one. This may prove successful, and by order the sagacious collie continues his task. Possibly the sheep may run away entirely, and, followed by the competitor, gallop until the latter is out of sight and out of hearing too. Then, after a tedious wait of a quarter of an hour or more, in the far distance the three sheep and their canine driver may be seen, the latter bringing his charge back to his owner, irrespective of course to be followed, or anything else. All he knows is that his duty is to fetch the sheep, and this he does.

Another difficulty comes when one of the three sheep cannot move as fast as the others, and, being hard pushed, ultimately gives up entirely and lies down; in which case the best dog in the world cannot make it rise again until thoroughly rested and so inclined. One batch of sheep may almost of themselves go the course, and require little driving by the dog, whilst, *au contraire*, another lot may be just as stupid and wayward, willing to be taken in any direction but the right one. Sometime the collie is unable to make a start at all through his perverse flock separating and trotting away in different directions immediately they are loosed from the liberation pen. Again the competitor may perform his driving task admirably, but is quite unable to consummate his work of making the sheep enter the pen at the end of the trial. Repeatedly at this penning the best work is shown, and the patience of the dog must be well supported by that of the shepherd.

To be successful at these trials the dog must be sagacious, well trained, quick of hearing, and sharp in his sight, patient, and have a peculiar power in commanding his sheep. That some collies possess the latter important qualification to a greater degree than others I am confident, and, although there is a considerable amount of good or bad fortune in obtaining an easy, or the reverse, batch of sheep, still the very best dogs appear to make even the most stupid little "Welshman" or "Scotchman" know that no larking will be allowed, and that they must go exactly where the dog wishes. This is a power similar to that possessed by some men over animals—the performer in the menagerie over his lions or tigers to wit—and in breeding collies for working I should certainly use those dogs which possessed this extraordinary and unusual gift to the greatest extent. A barking dog is useless at such meetings, and one that loses its temper, rushes at and attempts to bite his sheep is equally (or sooner) put out of the stake.

In training or practising a collie for work of this kind care must be taken that the lessons are given in both directions, *i.e.* the dog be taught to work from left to right and *vice versa*. I have seen an otherwise good dog make a wretched performance when it came to compete on a course which lay in a direction contrary to that in which its early lessons had been given. The most difficult thing to teach is to make your dog drive the sheep away from you—any duffer almost will bring them up to you, but taking them away altogether for a half a mile or so up to a certain point, and then turning them towards the home journey, requires great skill, more so than is required at the pen when the trial is terminating.

Quietly that shepherd there, a sturdy son of Cumberland, who spends forty weeks of the year amongst his flock, takes the piece of cord off his dog's neck which has done duty as chain and collar, and receives his instructions from the judges. The three sheep are liberated, Fan, a grey and white little bitch, pricks her ears and brightens her eyes, but does not leave the heels of her master. He snaps his fingers, " Hie to 'em, lass," and sharp as the arrow from the bow Fan bounds in front, steadies herself, looks around, spies a black head and a pair of curved short horns, and is behind her sheep in an instant. One might think, as the latter look wildly around, they would rush off in different directions. The wether stamps his foot, the young ewes press closer to him. Fan stops for orders with one eye on the sheep, the other on her worker; both ears sharply open to any sound from the latter. "Gang on!" calls the Cumbrian, and on goes the bitch to the sheep, who, staring at her a moment, see determination in her eyes and turn to flee. They try to separate, the collie bitch will not allow this, but keeps about five yards behind her minute flock, and, just as a good greyhound wrenches with his hare, moves to this side and to that as the sheep appear to incline one way or the other. "Git away!" is the cry that reaches Fan, who drives in a direction contrary to that from whence the order comes, and a mighty waving of the huge hands she sees as she looks around, and, obeying the command, sends the little flock, now under command, on the far side of the first flag. Proceeding, a sharp whistle or two keeps Fan at her task, and, as she too nearly approaches the near side of a second flag, "Away back!" is promptly obeyed, and this stage of the journey is safely accomplished, and a third signal mark is equally well rounded.

Now there comes a "sheep trod" or footpath used by the natives of the country, and up this the three sheep will go, totally oblivious of the duty they are expected to perform, and, fancying themselves on their own hills, gallop as hard as they can along the narrow road, Fan after them. A prolonged and shrill whistle from the shepherd causes the bitch to look back. A hand held up and Fan drops, like a steady setter that has just located game, and awaits further signal. The sheep eventually stop running, look around, one picks a mouthful of grass, another follows suit. That whistle again! up jumps the bitch and is away to her charge once more, and quietly and sensibly contrives to turn them off the path and drive them in the direction now indicated, right up to a stone fence in which an opening has been made and through which the sheep must go. Maybe they will, most likely they will not. A moment's hesitation, the bitch presses them a little and they bolt right up the fence side to the corner, from whence they refuse to budge, turning round and facing the dog once more. The shepherd gives his signal, and over the wall leaps Fan, is lost to sight a moment but re-appears on the top of the fence right above the sheep; who, alarmed by the apparition, forthwith return by the way they came. A loud cheer from the spectators testifies their appreciation of this excellent piece of work. Again the woolly stupids boggle at the opening in the fence (that "gap-steeād" the natives call it), but in due course are persuaded to go through and into the next allotment. Ordinary driving by signal and whistle is successfully accomplished along the remainder of the course to the boundary where the turn has to be made towards home. Sometimes the trial is here extended, and both sheep and dog disappear in the distance, but Fan, well-trained, is lucky in going no more than a score of yards or so behind the furthest flag, and a cheery "fetch 'em up" causes her to hurry the little flock towards the penning hurdles to which the shepherd now moves from his original position and awaits their coming.

Within these hurdles the sheep have to be placed before the trial ends successfully. John is a careful man and knows his work. He lays down his stick at one corner, and possibly divesting himself of his coat or plaid, places that on the top, whilst Fan is diligently bringing up her charge. There are the coat and stick at one side of the opening, John is at the other; Fan has to bring the sheep between the two. A seemingly easy task. The latter are suspicious and still wild; they look about them, ultimately turn, and, notwithstanding the furious antics of John in his shirt-sleeves, rush right past him, stop and look about them fifty yards away. Fan has dropped of her own free will, and lies crouched upon the grass. A moment to allow the trio to settle down somewhat; when up she springs by signal, and is soon behind them again. A second and a third time they break away, running around the pen as it they were looking for the opening, but at the same time always avoiding it. Now they are quiet, seemingly docile, with the entrance right in front. Fan has again crouched down. John has again spread out his arms—his wings they may be called—like some huge human butterfly. A sheep has its head almost in the opening. Fan crawls along on her belly; gradually she drives her charge forwards. One is in the pen, but, coming out again in an instant, does an unrehearsed circus performance around the hurdles. Fan has at last obtained the measure of its mates, will not allow them to move away, and the three are together once more. "Shoo! shoo-o!" says the shepherd, as he again expands his whitened arms—his wings; the sheep move a yard. Fan, on her belly, crawls two yards. Two feet, one foot more, and, huddling together in a heap, the three "black faces" jostle into the pen. Fan, on her feet in a moment, prevents their exit. John waves his hat to the judges, picks up his coat and stick, receives a signal that all is right, and so concludes the trial.

It has been a good one; and everybody says the patient, sturdy Cumbrian's clever little bitch will be "a deuced bad 'un to lick"; and, as a fact, she is, for she wins the first prize.

The three sheep are turned out of their temporary pen, and without difficulty John, with Fan at his heels, drives them off the ground, and the next competitor is called upon.

Such is a description of an ordinary trial, which, of course, may be considerably varied according to the nature of the ground over which it is run. Arrangements are generally made by which the puppies, that have usually a special stake for themselves, work over a shorter and easier course than the all-aged dogs, for reasons that will, naturally, be obvious. Although the time test, *i.e.*, the shortest time in which the task is performed, is not absolutely a criterion of the best work; some arrangement as to time must be made, and this is usually left to the discretion of the judges. Thus, if ten minutes (or a quarter of an hour) are allowed in which to perform the allotted work, any dog that occupies that time, either by losing or separating its sheep before half the work is completed, may be struck out altogether; and, as I have said, a similar penalty attaches where a dog bites his sheep or barks at them to any extent, further than perhaps an odd note or two when such may be absolutely required under extraordinary circumstances. The latter, when the sheep "take steck," as it were, and refuse to budge from a corner into which they may have run, or have sought refuge in a dried-up water-course, behind a stone heap or at any similar obstruction.

The judges at such gatherings as these must be either shepherds or farmers, some one actually and practically acquainted with the work required of dogs, a duty for which I need scarcely say the modern show judge is not by any means fitted. Most of the latter have never attended a collie trial meeting; many of them have never seen a sheep dog work, excepting so far as running after a carriage is concerned, or chasing a rabbit or killing a rat, when they have been specially trained for the purpose of such illegitimate duties.

Now, a word or two of the class, style, and character of the dogs that perform best at these trials with sheep; and I need scarcely say that as a rule the modern winner in the show-ring is not usually seen to advantage in such a position, although at times good-looking dogs, and well-bred ones, too, do creditable work. Mr. J. J. Steward, of Rugby, a breeder of prize collies of considerable repute, has occasionally successfully run dogs at some of the Welsh trials; his Smart by no means belying its name. Another of the best Welsh dogs was Dr. Edwards's black and tan Toss, who was very successful at many of the trials in the Principality—possibly the best animal, locally, of his generation. It was a great disappointment when Toss went into the North of England to compete with the leading dogs there, and quite failed to come up to the expectations formed of him. The sheep were different from those he had been accustomed to, whilst the air and general surroundings were not Welsh enough for him. From corresponding causes some of the best English dogs have not done well when competing in Wales. This dog Toss was a strong black and tan, with a profuse, correct coat, and so good looking generally, that in 1881, at Llangollen, he was handed the special prize given to the handsomest dog on the ground. Dr. Drinkwater's Boy was another excellent Welsh dog; and no less skilful were Mr. John Williams's Handy, Mr. Rigby's Smart, Mr. Evans's Lassie, Mr. Dempster's Tweed, and Mr. Michael Williams's Lass. Mr. J. Freme, Wepre Hall, Flint, for some time ran dogs with great success, and possessed excellent animals, his Jet being especially good.

I was unfortunately not present at the trials held near Llangollen in 1889, but I am informed that a dog that won one of the chief prizes, appeared to have as much setter blood in him as anything else, but his true breeding it would be difficult to define from appearance; still that day in August, he worked so well, that later on he was one of those selected to appear before Her Majesty under circumstances already alluded to. In the Royal presence, however, he quite failed to sustain his reputation; nor has he done so since.

Again, at the North of England trials, time after time peculiar-looking dogs are to be observed taking leading honours; some of the best workers I ever saw being wire-haired in coat, of an appearance likely to be brought about by crossing a shepherd's bitch with a rough terrier. But I was assured that these dogs were pure-bred sheep dogs, and had been such for generations. I suppose no better dog ever ran anywhere than Mr. Harding's (Caton, near Lancaster) Rob, an old-fashioned grey, grizzled stamp, that might from his appearance have had a dash of deerhound blood in him. He won many leading prizes, but was once or twice unfortunately beaten in the champion classes by

Mr. Martindale's Mite and by Mr. Barcroft's Trim. But all round I believe Rob was the best working sheep-dog I ever saw. Other good animals of a like pattern have been Mr. Barcroft's Nip, Mr. R. Huck's Corby, and Mr. R. W. Metcalf's Sep. None of these latter are, however, collies proper under the modern acceptation of the term, and so the leading meetings both in Wales and in the North of England are called. "sheep-dog trials," in order that any dog, irrespective of his strain, so long as he be properly trained and broken to work sheep, may compete. This is a very wise precaution in order to save trouble so far as objections are concerned. Any evil it might do to the breed by allowing cross-bred dogs to compete, is counteracted by the special prizes awarded to the handsomest dog on the ground whose work has been to the satisfaction of the judges.

At the Kirkby Stephen meeting in 1881, one of the handsome collies competed, Mr. F. Pott's (Brampton) Rob, then nine years old, but still possessing all that expression and character, with size and an excellent coat, required to win on the show bench. Performing his work very well indeed, under most unfavourable circumstances, he was not quite fast enough and sufficiently sharp and brisk to compete successfully against much younger animals, though he came second at Llangollen in 1872, and the judges there, as others had previously done at Kirkby Stephen, presented him with the beauty prize. Rob on this occasion was entered as belonging to Mr. Harding (Castle Carrock). Mr. R. Huck (Barrows Green, Westmoreland), also had a goodish looking bitch called Fly, a most successful and consistent performer in the field, both in England and Wales. She, however, appeared neither long nor short coated; had she possessed the shaggy jacket and good frill many worse workers owned, she would have won the " beauty cup" oftener than was the case. Mr. Martindale (Bendrigg), Westmoreland, had another handsome dog, a black and tan, called Milton, good enough to win both by field and bench. Mr. J. Akerigg, Mr. J. Ivison, Mr. J. S. Pattison, and Mr. R. Bracken, in addition to the farmers already named, have at times owned some highly-successful workers, both of the rough-coated and smooth-coated varieties.

During recent years Mr. J. Barcroft, of Scout Moor, Shuttleworth, Lancashire, appears to have devoted more time and money in endeavouring to obtain perfection in the working sheep dogs than anyone else. His efforts, too, have met with quite an average amount of success. The best dogs he has owned have been Bob, Trim, Sall, and Nip, the latter an active black and white little bitch, as sharp as a needle and more sensible than some human beings.

Dr. James (Kirkby Lonsdale), Mr. Steward, already mentioned, Mr. W. D. Inman (Coniston), and Mr. W. W. Thomson (Mitcham), seem to be about the only bench exhibitors of collies who have made entries at the sheep dog competitions. Mr. Lloyd Price has given them great support, and, as I have already stated, was one of their founders, and he at times does not deem it derogatory to his dignity as the head of a leading county family, to occasionally place some of his dogs (not collies however) within the magic circle of the show ring.

The surroundings of these trials are simple enough, and so are the rules for their conduct, and the following are the only ones in use at the old established Llangollen meeting. They may be found useful to those who wish to promote similar entertainments, as may those of the North Western Counties Association, which follow:

### LLANGOLLEN SHEEP DOG TRIALS—RULES.

1.—All Dogs entered for the Local Stakes must be on the ground at 8.30 a.m. Those for the Cambrian Stakes at 9.30 a.m., and, except when competing, must be held by cord or chain, under penalty of disqualification.

2.—No Dogs, except those competing, will be allowed on the **ground.**

3.—Any dog that injures a sheep will be disqualified, and the owner of the dog will be liable for the damage.

4.—No one will be allowed with the dog competing except the man working him, and he will be placed where the Committee direct.

5.—The Committee, with the assistance of the Judges, will decide the time to be allowed to each dog.

6.—The Judges have the power of ordering up as soon as they please any dog that commits a flagrant error, and their decision in all cases shall be final.

7.—In case of insufficient merit, the judges are empowered to withhold the prizes according to their discretion.

### NORTH WESTERN COUNTIES SHEEP DOG TRIALS ASSOCIATION REGULATIONS.

All dogs entered must have been not less than three months the *bond fide* property of the Exhibitor, and, except when competing, must be held by cord or chain, under penalty of disqualification.

Any competitor five minutes late after his name has been called will be disqualified, and his Entrance Fee forfeited.

No dogs, except those competing, will be allowed on the ground.

If three or more competitors so desire, the names of the dogs will be publicly drawn the day before the meeting actually takes place, and the dogs will be run in the order drawn.

If the entries exceed the number that the Committee consider

## Rules and Regulations. 119

can be run in one day, the Committee will draw by lot the dogs to be excluded in any stakes, but every possible effort and arrangement will be made to run all the dogs entered.

Any dog that injures a sheep will be disqualified, and the Owner of such dog will be liable for the damage.

Any competitor disobeying the Judges or any of the authorities will be disqualified.

No person will be allowed with the dog competing, except the man working him, and he will be placed where the Judges direct.

The Judges will decide as to the time the dogs will have allotted to do the work set out, and have the power of ordering up, as soon as they please, any dog that commits a flagrant error.

In cases of insufficient merit, the Judges are empowered to withhold the prizes according to their discretion.

The prize for the best-looking dog or bitch is only open to those who have competed in the trials to the satisfaction of the Judges.

The decision of the Judges shall on all points be final.

No dog entered for the Champion Stakes will be allowed to compete in any other class.

No dog will be allowed to compete in the All-aged or Local Stakes that has won a first prize given by this Association.

No dog will be allowed to compete in more than one class, except for the best-looking, and those entered in the Local Stakes.

Entries accompanied by the fees, must be delivered by post or otherwise, to one of the secretaries.

Entrance Fees for dogs not drawn, or rejected for any reason before the trials, will be returned.

In this chapter an endeavour has been made to convey some idea as to what trials with sheep dogs are, especially to those persons who are unacquainted therewith, and who may be desirous of introducing them into some locality where hitherto they have been unknown. The rules, too, of the leading associations are printed for a similar purpose, and I hope the whole may prove of interest and use to those for whom they have been written. A handsome collie dog is worth much gold; when in addition to beauty it possesses intelligence and obedience, obtained through shepherd's training, the value is enhanced incalculably, and the fortunate owner of such an animal possesses the most faithful four-footed companion in existence.

## CHAPTER VII.

The Collie Clubs — Their Standard of Excellence — Scales and Points — The Scottish Collie Club — Intelligence of the Collie — Some Anecdotes — Trained to Perform — Sheep Worrying.

THE COLLIE CLUB was established in 1881; strangely, its head-quarters have always been in London, and, until this year, a large majority of its Committee have resided in the South of England. Personally, I am not greatly in favour of these specialist dog clubs, for they too often drift into a certain groove, selecting their own judges from their own members, who, turn and turn about, come as it were to judge each other's dogs, as well as those of the general public. Perhaps, on the whole, the Collie Club has been far less faulty in this particular than other similar bodies, for its management has been satisfactorily conducted by a body of men whose conduct is above suspicion. Thus, the Club has maintained its success, now numbers some eighty members, and possesses a nice little balance at its banker's. Whether this Club has improved in the collie in the best manner possible may be disputed by some, but there is no getting away from the fact that, at its last show, there were more really first-rate young dogs shown than have been previously seen at any exhibition, and there was scarcely a bad one benched.

More might undoubtedly have been done with regard to the improvement of, and encouragement in the working of, the variety, but the first attempt in this direction under the auspices of the Club—those trials at the Alexandra Palace already alluded to—was by no means a success. How could it be, with such surroundings? A lot of wild Welsh sheep turned down amongst the laurel bushes and shrubs of a suburban pleasure ground! Everything was strange, even to the working of the dogs and to the awards of the prizes. Still the experiment might have been repeated amid more suitable surroundings, and any reproach that may rest on the Club, as to the improvement in the beauty of its favourite dog at the expense of its intellectual capacity, would have been removed.

Of course the Club has given us its description of the true type of collie, which is as follows:—

"The *skull* of the collie should be quite flat and rather broad, with fine tapering muzzle of fair length, and mouth the least bit overshot, the eyes widely apart, almond shaped and obliquely set in the head; the skin of the head tightly drawn, with no folds at the corners of the mouth; the ears as small as possible, semi-erect, when surprised or listening, at other times thrown back and buried in the 'ruff.'

"The *neck* should be long, arched, and muscular, the shoulders also long, sloping and fine at the withers; the chest to be deep and narrow in front, but of fair breadth behind the shoulders.

"The *back* to be short and level, with the loin rather long, somewhat arched and powerful. Brush long 'wi' upward swirl' at the end, and normally carried low.

"The *fore legs* should be perfectly straight with a fair amount of flat bone, the pasterns rather long, springy, and slightly lighter of bone than the rest of the leg; the foot with toes well arched and compact, soles very thick.

"The *hind-quarters*, drooping slightly, should be very long from the hip bones to the hocks, which should be neither turned inwards nor outwards, with stifles well bent. The hip bones should be wide and rather ragged.

"The *coat*, except on legs and head, should be as abundant as possible; the outer coat straight, hard and rather stiff, the under coat furry and so dense that it would be difficult to find the skin. The 'ruff' and 'frill' especially should be very full. There should be but little 'feather' on the fore legs, and none below the hocks on the hind legs.

"*Colour* immaterial.

"*Symmetry.*—The dog should be a fair length on the leg, and his movements wiry and graceful; he should not be too small, height of dogs from 22 to 24 inches, of bitches from 20 to 22 inches.

"The greyhound type is very objectionable, as there is no brain room in the skull, and with this there is to be found a fatuous expression, and a long powerful jaw.

"The setter type is also to be avoided, with its pendulous ear, full soft eye, heavily feathered legs, and straight short flag.

"The smooth collie only differs from the rough in its coat, which should be hard, dense, and quite smooth."

## Scale of Points.

| | |
|---|---|
| Head and expression | 15 |
| Ears | 10 |
| Neck and shoulders | 10 |
| Legs and feet | 15 |
| Hind quarters | 10 |
| Back and loins | 10 |
| Brush | 5 |
| Coat with frill | 20 |
| Size | 5 |
| **Total** | **100** |

NOTE.—Point judging is not advocated, but figures are only made use of to show the comparative value attached to the different properties; no marks are given for "general symmetry," which is, of course, in judging a point of the utmost importance.

Such we must take to be the accepted description of the collie dog as he is now admired on the show bench and kindly treated in his own home. There may be exceptions taken to some of the remarks, and without being thought hypercritical, I may say that the line as to colour being immaterial is at any rate misleading. Colour has a considerable amount of weight with all our judges, and there is not one who would place a really tip-top dog that was all white, over one a little less perfect in livery of the orthodox black, tan, and white, or the even handsomer rich red sable with a collar of white, and frill and tail tip to match. Nor would a brindled dog do, nor one brindled and black, nor one altogether black. Colour ought to have had, at any rate, five points given in the scale, for certainly they are allowed, although not prescribed. The back and loins, too, are hardly dealt with, for with but ten points allowed there, a cripple in his hind-quarters could win in the best of classes, were he perfect in other respects.

The following is the apportionment of points that might be adopted, though I, like those in authority, by no means advocate this point judging, a scale may be useful to amateurs in determining how far a seeming defect in their dog may be fatal to its success in the ring :

| | |
|---|---|
| Shape of head | 10 |
| Expression in eyes and face, with general carriage (character) | 18 |
| Ears | 10 |
| Neck and shoulders | 5 |
| Legs and feet | 15 |
| Back, loins, and hind-quarters | 15 |
| Brush or tail | 5 |
| Size | 5 |
| Coat, including colour, and frill | 17 |
| Total | 100 |

Weight for dogs from 50lb. to 60lb.; bitches from 40lb. to 50lb.

With some little appearance of an inclination for "home rule," our neighbours over the border have formed a Collie Club of their own, which they call the "Scottish Collie Club," and have taken considerable pains to draw up a description of their own, and made an apportionment of points. These are as follows, and readers will thus be able to compare them with the points and descriptions that have come before:

"ROUGH-COATED.

"*Head* moderately long in proportion to the dog's size, covered with short soft hair. Skull flat, moderately wide between the ears, and gradually tapering to the eyes. There should be a very slight elevation of the eyebrows, and very little stop.

"*Muzzle* of fair length, tapering to the nose, which, whatever the colour of the dog, should be black. The teeth, which are white and of good size, should not be over nor undershot. Both are faults, the latter the greater of the two.

"*Eyes*, of fair size, but not prominent, are placed rather close together, and set obliquely in the head, which gives that cunning foxy expression so characteristic of the breed. Colour, any shade of brown, the darker the better, yellow eyes being a great fault. Dogs of a mirled colour should have a mirled or china eye, and sometimes both eyes are of this colour.

"*Ears* small, placed rather close together at the top of the head, covered with short soft hair, and carried semi-erect when at attention; at other times thrown back, and buried in the frill.

"*Neck* long, arched, and muscular.

"*Body* rather long than short, ribs well rounded, chest deep and narrow in front, but of a fair breadth behind the shoulders, which should be oblique. Loin rather long, and slightly arched, showing power.

"*Legs*.—Fore legs straight and muscular, with a fair amount of flat bone, the fore-arm moderately fleshy, the hind legs less fleshy, very sinewy, and hocks well bent. Pasterns long and light in bone. Feet oval in shape, the soles well padded, and the toes well arched and close.

"*Tail*, moderately long, carried low when the dog is quiet, gaily when excited, and almost straight out when running.

"*Coat*.—This is a very important point. The coat, except on the head and legs, should be abundant, the outer coat harsh to the touch, the inner coat soft and furry, and very close, so close that it is difficult on parting the hair to see the skin. The hair very abundant round the neck and chest; this is termed the frill. The mask is smooth, the fore legs slightly feathered, the hind legs below the hocks smooth. Hair on tail very profuse, and on the hips long and bushy.

"*Colour*.—Any colour.

"*Size*.—Dogs 21 to 24 inches at shoulder, bitches 2 inches less.

"*Weight*.—Dogs 45lb. to 60lb., bitches 40lb. to 50lb.

"*General Appearance*.—A lithe active dog, with no useless timber about him, his deep chest showing strength, his sloping shoulders, and well-bent hocks speed, and his "bawsint" face high intelligence. The face should bear a sharp, doubtful expression. As a whole, he should present an elegant and pleasing outline, quite distinct from any of our other domesticated breeds, and show great strength and activity.

"*Faults*.—Domed skull, high peaked occipital bone, heavy pendulous ears, full soft eyes, heavy feathered legs, short tail."

## Scale of Points.

| | |
|---|---|
| Head | 15 |
| Eyes | 5 |
| Ears | 10 |
| Neck and shoulders | 10 |
| Body | 10 |
| Legs and feet | 15 |
| Tail | 5 |
| Coat | 20 |
| Size and general appearance | 10 |
| Total | 100 |

### Smooth-Coated.

"The smooth collie only differs from the rough in its coat, which should be hard, dense, and quite smooth."

The general expression of the rough-coated collie is intelligent, kindly, crafty, and bright; when he erects his ears and looks up into your face for orders, his dark eyes seem, as it were, to speak, his lips twitch, his mouth almost open, for were he possessed of human power and voice, he would say "What do you want now, bothering me and rousing me from pleasant dreams?" He is the most companionable of all dogs; when properly trained the most obedient, the most faithful, a clever watch and guard, particularly skilful in distinguishing friend from foe. He readily undertakes to perform any work for which he is intended, and can be broken to track a wounded deer almost as easily as to guard and drive a flock of sheep.

One writer tells us that a Scotch shepherd's lad and an intelligent collie can destroy as many grouse before the season comes in as the lessee will shoot during his time of occupation.  Indeed, so intelligent is this dog that too often he is trained to evil deeds, and becomes a confirmed poacher.  Worse, too, has happened to him, for he has been turned into a sheep stealer.  His wicked owner during the daytime was in the habit of looking over any flock of sheep from which he wished to make his thefts. Those selected, were pointed out to his dog, and, in the night, the faithful collie was sent into the field or on to the common, and never failed to drive from the flock those very sheep that had been pointed out to him during the day.  This went on for a considerable time till the fellow was caught, tried, I believe at Carlisle, when, on being found guilty, he confessed to the part his well-trained and sagacious dog had in the crime.  The man was hanged, but what became of the dog the chronicler does not state.

There are admirers of the sheep dog who believe he can tell almost to a word what is said to him.  " I'm thinking, sir! the cow is in the potatoes," says the shepherd to Mr. Charles St. John, and, though no aspiration is laid upon the words, up jumps the dog, which had seemingly been asleep, but with one ear open, runs out at the door, comes back, looks up in his master's face as if to say, " All right, you have been making a fool of me! the cow is not in the potatoes," and curls himself up once more.  Who could say that this dog did not understand the words his master used, although they came out during the general conversation?

Mr. J. H. Walsh ("Stonehenge") in his Dogs of the British Isles, tells a story very much to the same point. He says:

" A curious case, which a short time ago happened to

myself, would almost lead to the belief that the collie understands the meaning of a conversation between members of the human family. Entering the drawing-room of a lady who has a celebrated dog of this variety as a pet, I was met with the question, 'What do you think of my dog? is he not a perfect beauty?' After looking him over as he lay on the rug, and with a desire to teaze my hostess, to whom I owed a Rowland or two for her previous many Olivers administered in badinage, I replied, very quietly, ' Yes, certainly, if he had but a collie coat and a little more ruff.' The words were hardly out of my mouth than the dog rose from his recumbent position, seized one of my feet in his mouth, gave it a gentle but vicious little shake, not sufficient to scratch the leather of my boot, and then lay down again. There was no emphasis on my part, and not a word uttered by the lady until after the act was completed, when I need scarcely say that eyes and tongue told me that I was rightly served. Anyhow, it was a remarkable coincidence, and from a long knowledge of the dog I really am inclined to believe that G—— knew I was 'picking holes in his coat,' and resented the injustice accordingly. Possibly, as in many human beings, he prides himself most on his only weak point, being absolutely perfect in every other and not much amiss there."

One could re-produce stories by the score as to the sagacity of this dog, many of them true, some no doubt otherwise. Of late years I have repeatedly seen performing collies on the stage and in the circus ring, and although they, as a rule, go through their tricks well and with precision, they are excelled by the poodle. One I observed at a certain place of entertainment which turned summersaults fairly well; another trainer, "Professor" Patterson, had one that walked on a barrel and across a so-called tight rope; the latter feat achieved with the addition of a monkey being carried on the dog's back. About the same time a Mr. Harris, connected with a large exhibition at Olympia, London, had a collie which usually gave its performances privately. These, which consisted of selecting named cards from a pack, and other tricks, were so extraordinary that the daily papers announced that a special performance was given before H.R.H. the Prince of Wales.

There is no doubt that the collie can be trained to any purpose whatever; he at times makes a fair retriever, and the best all-round dog for shooting over I ever owned was a collie with a slight dash of retriever blood in him. As already stated, his intelligence can be turned to bad account, and sometimes this is done of his own free will, when he becomes a confirmed sheep worrier. This evil is often brought about by the custom of shepherds allowing the dead lambs to remain unburied; and the same is often done with the sheep themselves. Indeed, I have seen a farmer's son go into the fields and find a sheep that has not long been dead, take it on his back down to the homestead, and there skin and "butch" it, all in the presence of the dog, who now and then is thrown a bit of the defunct sheep. From this he speedily gets a taste for raw flesh, and if he cannot find a dead sheep upon which to satisfy his craving, comes to kill one for himself. The farmer's household salt the "found dead," hang it up, make it into a "ham," and eat it themselves. This meat in Scotland and the north of England, and, perhaps, elsewhere, is known as "braxy," in the south of England as "dropped mutton." One authority says that those shepherd's dogs that are adepts at marking sheep lost and covered over in snow drifts are liable to become sheep worriers, and in the summer months are the devourers of those poor creatures of whom they may have been the saviours during the winter. This may be so, but personally I have traced many cases which undoubtedly arise from the causes I have already named. If sheep-worrying collies were confined only to those that had an opportunity of saving lives in the snow, they would not have been nearly so numerous as was the case twenty or thirty years ago. Farmers and shepherds take care to bury their dead lambs and sheep nowadays.

When the sheep dog does become a confirmed sheep killer, his sagacity is apparent in a remarkable degree. Mr. W. Dickinson, in "Cumbriana," gives some interesting notes on this subject. He says: "The sheep dog is entitled to the credit of being the cleverest of the dog tribe, as a sheep destroyer, for he goes about his work more cunningly than any other of his race, and is seldom found out before much harm is done. In cases many months have elapsed before the culprit is detected, so wary has he been in all his proceedings. He takes his victim by the throat, overturns, and throttles it at once. He is seldom known to worry near home, or among the flock of his owner. When once blooded, he will sneak two or three miles away in the dark to a strange flock, and will sometimes entice a youngster with him, both attacking the same sheep; the older animal at the throat, the younger wherever it can lay hold of. In its excitement the young dog is apt to give an occasional bark, but the older one never barks at all.

"The sheep dog usually begins his sport about midnight, and after a lively hour or so of destructive amusement, rolls and rubs himself on the grass, and is found at home in the morning as clean and tidy and unconcerned as if he had been all night in his kennel, or sleeping at the foot of the straw rick."

The same writer considers that, as a rule, the sheep dog perpetrates these crimes for mere amusement, and this may be so in some few instances, but even where the same dog kills three or four lambs in a single night, he will have regaled himself with a small *bonne bouche* from the carcase of each, as well as lapping a good proportion of their blood. Then, again, some of the sheep may have been smothered by being huddled up in a heap together through fear, or may be, the dog becomes alarmed, and, like the disturbed thief, bolts without being able to profit by his plunder.

Another little story bearing on this unsavoury subject, and I have done. An angling friend of my acquaintance (the late Mr. G. F. Braithwaite, of Kendal, author of some charming papers on fishing matters), told me that one day he was walking along the road to get to the banks of the river Lune, near Tebay, accompanied by a farmer, who had, of course, his shepherd's dog at his heels. Another shepherd's dog, unaccompanied, came trotting along the road, and the two collies fraternised by wagging their tails and smiling, for dogs can smile, and rubbing their noses together. Mr. Braithwaite noticed something peculiar about the friendship of these dogs, so stopped, and was surprised to see the one alone go on its way, whilst that with his friend turned back and set off in the direction from which the strange dog had come.

"Why! What means this?" said the fisherman, "Your dog has gone home!" "Nay, nay," replied the farmer, "that dog as came to us has been feedin' on a dead sheep up on 't fells, and 'Beaut' (his dog's name) has just gone back to hev' a feed on it hersel', an' we'll not see her back much afore night." This is how our faithful friends become transformed into murderers, and here was a strange instance of communication of ideas between two dumb creatures, for when "Beaut" did come home at night it was to sleep off the effects of a barbarous carouse, and, no doubt, the dogs would return to their repast so long as the crows and ravens left a particle of flesh upon the bones.

One remarkable thing in the two varieties of collie, the rough and the smooth coated, is that, unlike what occurs with the two varieties of fox terriers and the rough and smooth-coated St. Bernards, where both sorts may be produced from one litter, I have never known of perfectly smooth and rough collie dogs from the same parents. The huge St. Bernard is particularly liable to do this, and our present champion (Sir Bedivere), who is long or rough-coated, has a litter brother called Baron Wallasey, who competes successfully in the smooth or short-haired division. Many of our leading fox terriers, too, both smooth and rough, are more than cousins by courtesy.

I find little or no consanguinity between the two varieties of collie. The two will, of course, breed together, but it speaks well for the care taken in the production of both that the strains have not been allowed to become intermixed—a course that would no doubt prove detrimental to both.

Allusion has been made in an earlier chapter to the allegations that our modern sheep dogs, or some of them, were originally crossed with the Gordon or black and tan setter. My opinion is that no variety of dog in the British Isles can boast of purer blood, or possibly blood so pure, as that to which this volume is dedicated. Ever since he has been with us his services have been valued and useful; he has usually been kept for one purpose alone, and to cross him with greyhound, setter, or bull dog would have been to completely spoil him for the work for which he was or is required. The gay colours, the profuse coats, the long heads, the narrow skulls, and other exaggerated points have been obtained by careful selection and breeding, and not by the surreptitious introduction of "foreign blood" of either one kind or another. The modern collie is as pure a bred dog as we have, and will, no doubt, continue to be so to the end of his days.

## CHAPTER VIII.

Management — Rearing Puppies — Food — Bedding — Simple Ailments and Disorders — Preparing for Show — Conclusion.

SOME few notes as to the management of the collie dog when he is kept as a companion, or for the purposes of exhibition. Those who keep him on the farm and for work will require no such instructions. Most likely the first collie an ordinary individual possesses is a puppy he has obtained from some friend, or mayhap purchased it from a dealer. If possible, it is best to rear this in the country until it is six or eight months old, where a plenitude of fresh air can be had, and unlimited exercise. In any case it ought to have both, and from the time it is weaned, say at six weeks old, from four to six meals a day. Little and often being an excellent motto upon which to rear puppies until they begin to grow their canine teeth, which will show when the youngster is some five months or so old. Gradually the meals may be lessened in number until maturity is reached, when two a day are sufficient, and upon which dogs thrive better than upon only one.

## A Good Diet.

Bread and milk form the best diet as a commencement, but even from the very first an occasional crust, a little piece of fish, and a dry bone to gnaw at, will be found useful. When the puppy is put out to walk with a cottager or elsewhere, from one and sixpence to two shillings a week is usually paid, or say three shillings for two. Odd as it may seem, two puppies do better and are far less trouble than a single one. They play together, sleep together, and, that which is better than all, keep each other out of mischief, and are not so likely to get petted and pampered as where one is by itself. The latter is often nursed and cuddled to keep him from whining. If these puppies are required as companions, they must be reared in the house, and, though so young when taken from their dams, soon prove apt pupils with regard to cleanliness.

When four months old or so, even earlier if it be thought desirable, they may be initiated into the mysteries of chain and collar, the latter being worn continuously for a few days before the chain is brought into operation. This chain should have a swivel at each end, and one in the centre, they prevent the links from twisting and kinking if the puppy struggles. An excellent plan is, to contrive to make the puppy connect the chain with a nice ramble in the country, by keeping him shut up for some hours before it is fastened to the collar. When released, adjust the chain and set out for your walk, enticing the pupil along, and if needs be rewarding him with a piece of bread whenever he ceases to strain and pull in his endeavours to go in a contrary direction to the one you wish. With ordinary care, after a couple of lessons the puppy will come running to you whenever you dangle the chain, for it reminds him of the run out and possible reward. There is nothing more unpleasant to see than a full grown dog with his tail between his legs, half dragged, being forced along by his fair mistress. Moreover, in the show ring, a dog that is fond of being on the chain, will look to advantage, frisk about, and be so lively as to considerably enhance his chance of winning a prize. As a fact, a dog that "shows badly" on the chain, gives very little opportunity to the judge to discern his good qualities. On more than one occasion I have won a prize with a puppy inferior in quality to others he competed against, for the very reason that mine, being pleased to be on the chain, exhibited himself to the very best advantage.

However, before entering your dog at a show held under Kennel Club Rules—and most canine exhibitions now take place under them—he must be given a name and registered. The fee for this is one shilling, to be sent to the Secretary, Kennel Club, Cleveland-row, St. James', London. This done, and the name given (if not already selected by someone else; if it is you must make a fresh choice) is your own, and the dog can be sent to any show. Of course if your favourite is not intended for exhibitions, or if at some local show only, there is no need to make the registration, though there is an air of importance about it cheap at the "low price of one shilling."

The dog when he has grown all his canine teeth may be fed twice a day on food as various as possible, dog biscuits (dry or soaked), bread, milk, gravy, liver, fish, scraps from the house, vegetables, with occasionally sheep's paunches boiled, are by far the best, with, of course, plenty of bones. A dog like the collie requires abundant exercise and long rambles, even repeated walks in the streets will be found extremely beneficial to his good health and well being. If he sleeps in a stable, or in an outbuilding, a bed of dry pitch pine shavings, which may be obtained from your joiner or carpenter, are to be recommended, and other wood shavings are preferable to straw. Recently there has been introduced to the public very fine shavings for the purpose of bedding dogs called Sanus Litter. This appears to answer its purpose very well indeed, and, moreover, come in handily to pack up bottles and glass, which you may wish to send anywhere by carrier or rail. If straw or hay be used for bedding, a little " Sanitas," or Jeyes' disinfectant, scattered thereon keeps all things sweet, and prevents an accumulation of insects. Do not wash your collie often, for too much soap and water softens the coat, changes its texture; and, as a fact, gives it a less healthy appearance than if his cleanliness had been obtained by clean bedding, fresh air, rolling on the grass, or a swim in the river or pond.

An excellent plan, in rearing your puppies, is to give them in milk, about once a fortnight, a small teaspoonful of magnesia, until they are about four months old, when this may be changed for half of one of the "dog pills" sold by Hind, Chemist, Kendal. The latter, I and others have used on various breeds of dogs for years, with great satisfaction, they appear to give a healthy tone to the stomach, and so the usual attack of distemper is rendered less virulent and dangerous than would be the case had the medicine not been given.

Worms are a usual cause of death in puppies, and if they do not produce fatal complications they often retard their growth, produce an abnormal appetite, and cause the animal to be ill at ease, and staring and rough in its coat. To prevent this, as much as possible, 10 to 25 grains of newly ground areca nut may be given to the young puppies, according to their age, followed in a couple of hours by a dessert-spoonful of castor oil and buckthorn. The nut must, however, be given on an empty stomach, the patient having just previously been kept without food for from ten to twelve hours. The most successful and simple vermifuge for an ordinary full grown collie is 1 drachm of newly powdered areca nut and 2 grains of santonine, given in broth or mixed as a bolus, followed in three hours by a large table-spoonful of buckthorn and castor oil. In this case the patient must have been kept without food for twenty-four hours prior to the medicine being given. It is well to repeat this a second time after a week's interval.

I do not here intend to enter into any, learned or otherwise, disquisition on canine diseases, for there are many works which treat them fully, carefully, and practically, but there are sundry little disorders incident to the canine race which must be mentioned, and first and foremost comes distemper. Almost every kennelman and huntsman has his pet remedy for this complaint, which annually carries off thousands of puppies, an especially large number succumbing from the more or less unhealthy surroundings of dog shows to which they have been sent before their time. Personally, I would not allow a dog under twelve months old to be exhibited at all, unless it were at one of the open air gatherings of the Agricultural Societies, which open at ten o'clock and close at three or four o'clock on the same day. Mr. Everett Millais is taking a great interest in the exhibition of puppies, especially so far as disinfecting the show benching is concerned—but the remedy of total exclusion is the best of all. Moreover, showing these puppies tends to make breeders force them in their growth, and often enough, especially in the variety to which this volume is dedicated, have we seen unnaturally grown puppies winning even in the all-aged classes, which when matured have proved but sorry specimens. No doubt this has led the Collie Club to make their classes according to the age of the exhibits, those under twelve months old, under two years old, and over the latter age, competing in separate and distinct groups. This arrangement applies to no other variety of dog.

However; to our distemper. This disorder occurs in such various forms, and may be attended by so many complications that no one remedy can avail in all cases. If severe, the nearest veterinary surgeon should be called in immediately, but ordinary cases may be cured by the remedy advertised by Spratt's Patent, that should be kept handy for cases of emergency. One old gamekeeper I was acquainted with placed every reliance on a bolus of tar about the size of a small walnut, which he would give to his spaniels or retrievers directly the first symptoms appeared. Others I know are equally confident in the curative powers of Frank Gillard's specific. As I have said, puppies reared on the lines suggested seldom suffer very severely from distemper, and, during one period of ten years, when rearing a large number of puppies, I never lost a single one from this so often fatal complaint, and the worst attack in my kennel I traced to my folly in exhibiting a puppy at one of the four days' shows. That was a lesson to me I shall never forget.

Mange of one kind or another may occur through negligence; and, as prevention is far better than cure, cleanliness, with regular exercise and dietary, minimise the chances of such an outbreak. A useful remedy for ordinary red mange, one which can easily be compounded by the local chemist, is as follows:—" Olive oil and oxide of zinc, each 1 ounce; tincture of arnica, 3 drachms; water 8 ounces, to be gently used on the sore places about three times daily. The ointment, green iodide of mercury, 1½ drachms to 1½ ounces of lard, is likewise good, though I prefer the former. A dose of Epsom salts, about as much as will lie on a shilling, each morning in addition to either will hasten recovery. Another simple and excellent remedy for ordinary mange is composed of 6 ounces solution of sulphate of iron; water 1 pint; the affected parts to be fomented therewith twice daily. Fowler's solution of arsenic may be prescribed with great advantage in the case of skin disease, and, so long as ordinary care be observed, there is little or no danger in giving even comparatively large doses. It must, however, always be taken with the meals, and the most successful results are gained by gradually increasing the dose. Thus begin with say three drops a day sprinkled on the food, adding one drop daily until ten drops are given. If there appear unusual signs of listlessness in the dog, and his eyes become bloodshot, discontinue the drops altogether for a week, and then recommence with the small dose. This treatment carefully followed will cure even the most obstinate cases. A mixed, wholesome diet, including only a fair proportion of meat, is best whilst the dog is under the influence of the medicine. Of the various advertised lotions, that prepared by Elias Bishop in almost all cases proves perfectly successful, and it possesses a great advantage, being thoroughly cleanly and simple in its application.

Canker in the ear is a common ailment, often brought on by damp and neglect, always troublesome to cure if allowed to run too long without being attended to. The early symptoms are easily discernible by the animal shaking his head and rubbing his ears with his paws. Of course he may do this from the presence of some foreign substance having accidentally got into the ear, which, however, seldom happens. If canker is appearing, a slight redness or inflammation will be seen on examining the inside of the ear, whilst the outside likewise will be found unduly warm, even feverish. Wash the ear out carefully with luke warm water, allowing it to freely enter the passages, which is easily done by holding the head on one side. In an hour after doing this, having let the ear dry without allowing the patient to shake his head, apply the following lotion (in the same manner as the water had been used) three times daily: Alum. 5 grains; vinegar, 1 drachm; water, 1 ounce. Follow these directions carefully and a cure will result, The latter will possibly be hastened by morning doses of Epsom Salts; whilst light food, bread, and scraps from the house form the best regimen.

As I have said so much about the simpler ailments from which collies, like other dogs, are so often sufferers, the remarks may be made more complete by a slight reference to rabies, of which I was reminded by receiving, in my connection with *The Field*, the following note from "R. J." (King's Lynn): "I was out shooting only last Wednesday with a small spaniel, an excellent one, and who appeared very well then. On Thursday morning I noticed a great weakness in her hind legs, and later on a most copious discharge of mucus, which hung in lengths of three or four inches on each side of the mouth, and which was so tenacious that I could hardly wipe it off. She had also a great difficulty in swallowing anything. On Friday I sent it to a man who has had great experience with dogs. It had not been at his place long before it was seized with a violent fit, and would doubtless have bit him had he been unprepared. It had several more fits, and yesterday it was destroyed. In the summer it had a habit of snapping at flies, and I noticed several times last week it would go into corners and snap in the same way, although no flies were about. On the Saturday and Sunday morning it took no notice of me, and did not seem to recognise me. I should much like to know your opinion of the case. Was it general paralysis, do you think? The dog had had distemper."

Here was an instance of rabies in the most pronounced form, which an expert would recognise without any difficulty. Professor Brown says: " The history of the case proves beyond all doubt that an experienced sportsman may not only observe the symptoms, but realise their character so well as to be able to describe them with as much accuracy of detail as would be expected of a practised canine pathologist, without at any moment entertaining the least suspicion that he was dealing with a rabid dog. The mischief which the animal may have done would be in some measure compensated if every sportsman and owner of dogs in the kingdom could commit R. J.'s letter to memory, or, at least, hang a copy of it in some conspicuous place for the benefit of himself and his friends." Such being the opinion of one of our most eminent veterinary surgeons, I thought I could not do better than act on his suggestion and republish the note and his comments in the most conspicuous place over which I had control.

As to preparing a collie for show, that dog with the greatest amount of exercise and good food will always look brightest and best in his coat, and require the least amount of attention and grooming. Already I have said that too much washing softens the coat, and a similar effect is produced by over-grooming. The brush or comb may be used on the frill and coat to a limited extent; they bring out the "mane" to perfection, and prevent matted growth of coat which is so often seen on the hind-quarters and about the ears, and the latter stand out better and appear of smaller size where particular attention is paid to the hair about their roots. Any of the dog soaps may be used when the dog is washed the day before going to a show.

Some persons wash their collies two days before the exhibition takes place; others do not wash them at all, simply giving clean bedding daily prior to their exhibition.

One animal will look better under the one *régime*, a second under the other, and the exhibitor must use his own judgment under the circumstances. The washing is best done by having the dog standing in a tub or wooden utensil made for the purpose with lukewarm water reaching up to his belly; he can thus be thoroughly drenched and soused. Care must be taken to keep the water and the washing off the head of the subject until all the body is thoroughly completed. Dogs do not like their heads wet, and if you commence on the head the creature remains uncomfortable during the whole of the time he is undergoing the ordeal. "Elbow grease" is almost as good as soap during this tubbing operation, and dry him as thoroughly as possible before allowing him to go on to his bed or kennel. Hand rubbing and a stiff brush will give the finishing touches and make the dog tidy enough and fit to go before any judge in the land. When in the ring see that you show the dog and not yourself. The latter is often done by the exhibitor walking round with his own person between the eyes of the judge and his dog. This may be vanity—it always look foolish, and the spectators remark thereon.

In other varieties of *canis familiaris*, one hears a great deal as to trimming and "faking," the latter a slang expression for improving a dog by unnatural means, such as dyeing him to change his colour, pulling out his coat to alter his appearance, cutting his ears to make them hang properly, or operating upon his tail for a similar purpose. Happily for the good name of this most faithful collie dog, he requires very little tampering with or manipulating for the show. His ears at the roots may be trimmed by the removal of hair to a certain degree, and his frill can perchance be improved and increased by grooming, and no exception need be taken to such ordinary and innocent means as these. But cases have been where the tail of the collie has been cut underneath, in order that it might hang down brush-like, and not be carried curled into the hair of the back, as is customary with the Esquimaux dog and the Pomeranian. Of course such a proceeding as this is thoroughly illegal, especially as so many of our collies have had a great liking to so gaily carry their brushes. A much simpler remedy is to take a stick into the ring when you show a dog with such a defect, and as he erects his stern give him a reminder on the back that he is to put his tail between his legs. However, take care that this is done when the judge is not looking, for if he be a just judge he will at once order you to put your stick down; if a severe one you are politely requested to leave the ring. Possibly it is best in the long run to let your collie carry his profusely feathered brush in the manner most comfortable to himself and most conformable with his own dignity.

A great deal might be written of judges and judging, and

## A Good Character.

as to the behaviour when in the ring of both exhibitors and officials. In no case is it "good form" to smoke either pipe, cigar, or cigarette, any more than it is for one exhibitor to try to display the good points of his dog to the disadvantage of an opponent. A quarrelsome, fighting animal is quite out of place here. Such a one never looks well, a judge cannot observe its excellences when in a state of excitement, and ill temper and pugnacity are quite out of place in any collie, either in the show or at the sheep fold. Moreover, an excitable dog will set others off in a similar line, or maybe cow the shy ones, making them drop their ears and appear as sheepish as the flocks they are supposed to guard and drive. I know that many judges look with suspicion upon that man who enters the ring with a stick in one hand, the chain of his dog in the other. Why will be obvious from what has already been written. Here is a little experience : Some ten years ago I was judging the collies of a certain show, and having weeded out the inferior specimens, was puzzling as to three or four others for the first prize. The owner of one carried a cane. "Will you kindly discard the stick?" said I. " Certainly," was the reply. " Walk your dog across the ring, please." Up went the tail, curved right into the back, and the competition ended by that dog failing to take the chief prize Two years later I saw the same animal; then he could not raise his stern on a level with his loins, but he was winning first prizes and became a champion in due course. Need I suggest the tail had been operated upon.

Whether the introduction and popularisation of dog shows have benefited the collie I will leave my readers to surmise; that they have increased his value is beyond doubt. Few will deny that his disposition has been improved by his recognition in polite circles as a fashionable beauty, and the numbers that are seen in our popular suburbs and in the streets form proof that his popularity is not on the wane. Well, he is a good dog for the lady or gentleman to keep as a companion, and a useful one for the farmer and shepherd in their work. Neither of the latter could do without him. Thus he is valued in a double sense, and so less likely to have his place usurped by the uncouth Great Dane and the quaint Schipperke from foreign countries. Treat him well and make a friend of him, and the collie will requite your kindness. The more he sees of his owner the better he will understand him, and, brought up and reared on the lines I have endeavoured to suggest, no dog is so well fitted for his position in life as a handsome, elegantly marked collie. He is a picture in the sitting room or library, and a companion in the country.

## ADDENDA.

THE COLLIE CLUBS: THEIR RULES AND REGULATIONS.

ALLUSION has already been made to the Collie Club, which, established in 1881, has taken an initiative in popularising the breed by holding shows at stated intervals. Its scope might, however, be extended with advantage, and well conducted meetings for the trials of shepherds' dogs with sheep on lines similar to such as are periodically held in Wales, the North of England, and elsewhere, but taking place in the southern or midland counties, would, I am certain, be popular. Scotland, too, has its Collie Club, and there are, likewise, the Old English Sheep Dog Club and one or two minor bodies more or less of a local character.

The officials of the Collie Club are as follows: Honorary President—Mr. S. E. Shirley; the Rev. Hans F. Hamilton, Mr. F. Gaskell, Mr. W. H. Ralph, Mr. J. J. Steward, Mr. F. Wake-Walker, Mr. A. L. Chance, Mr. J. A. Doyle, Mr. H. L. While, Mr. W. P. Arkwright, Mr. W. R. Dockrell, Mr. G. R. Krehl, the Rev. Charles Kent, Mr. C. H. Megson, Mr. T. C. Stretch. Hon. Secretary and Hon. Treasurer— Mr. Alex. N. Radcliffe, 20, Craven-street, Charing-cross, London, W.

The Rules and Regulations of the Club are as follows :

1. *Name and Objects.*—The name of the club shall be "The Collie Club," and its objects shall be to promote the breeding of pure collies, to define precisely and publish a description of the true type, and to urge the adoption of such type on breeders, judges, dog show committees, &c., as the only recognised and unvarying standard by which collies are to be judged, and which may in future be uniformly accepted as the sole standard of excellence in breeding and in awarding prizes of merit in collies, and (by giving prizes, supporting shows, encouraging sheep dog trials, and taking other steps) to do all in its power to protect and advance the interests of the breed.

2. *Qualification of Members.*—The club shall consist of an unlimited number of members, whose names and addresses shall be kept by the secretary in a book, which book shall be open to the inspection of members at reasonable times. Any person favourable to the objects of the club shall be eligible for admission as a member, with the exception of professional dealers.

3. *Management of Club.*—Subject to the powers exercisable by general meetings of the club, the entire control and management of the club shall be vested in a committee of twelve and a president, to be elected from the general body of the members of the club, in the manner hereinafter provided. In all of these rules in which the committee is referred to (except in those relating to their retirement and election), that term shall be deemed to include the president.

4. *Election of Members.*—The election of members shall be vested solely in the committee, and be made by ballot, three members of the committee to be a quorum at such ballot, and two black balls to exclude.

5. Each candidate for admission shall be proposed by one member of the club personally known to him, and seconded by another also personally known to him.

6. *Subscription.*—The entrance money on admission to the club shall be £2 2s., and the annual subscription shall be £2 2s., payable on the 1st of January in each year. Any one failing to pay his subscription before the 1st of January shall have notice given him by the secretary, and if his subscription be still unpaid

on the 31st of March, his rights of membership shall cease, and he shall be struck off the list of members of the club.

7. *Withdrawal of Members.*—It shall be competent for any member to withdraw from the club on giving notice to the secretary (such member retiring to have no claim whatever on the club), provided always that such member shall be liable for his subscription to the club for the current year in which he gives such notice.

8. *Expulsion of Members.*—Any member violating the rules and regulations of the club for the time being in force shall be liable to be expelled by the committee, and any member of the club who shall be proved to the satisfaction of the committee to have in any way misconducted himself in connection with dogs or dog shows, or to have in any way acted in opposition to the fundamental rules and principles upon which the club has been established, or in any other manner which would make it undesirable that he should continue to be a member, shall be requested to retire from the club, and if a resolution to that effect shall be carried by three-fourths of the committee present at the meeting, the member so requested to retire shall thenceforth cease to be a member of the club as if he had resigned in the usual course, and his subscription for the current year shall be returned to him, and he shall be reported to the Kennel Club with a view to his being disqualified from showing at any show held under Kennel Club Rules, and from competing for prizes offered by the club.

9. *General Meeting.*—A general meeting of the club shall be held once at least in every year, at such time and place as the committee shall appoint, and eight members of the club shall be a quorum for such meeting. At least 21 days' notice of every general meeting shall be given to every member of the club.

10. The committee may at any time, and they shall, upon a requisition signed by any six members of the club, and specifying the business for which such meeting is required, summon a general meeting of the club. If within 21 days after the receipt of any such requisition the committee do not summon a general meeting, the requisitionists or any other six members of the club may do so.

11. Every general meeting shall be competent to elect members of committee in place of those retiring in rotation, to elect an

honorary president and honorary members without entrance fee or subscription, to consider and vote upon any report of the committee, and any resolution of which notice shall have been given to the members at least 14 days before the meeting. The committee shall be bound to give effect to any resolution which shall be adopted by a majority of the members present and voting.

12. At every general meeting the president of the club shall be chairman, or failing him a member of the committee, chosen by themselves; or, if there be no member of committee willing to take the chair, a chairman shall be elected by the majority of the members present.

13. The voting at all general meetings shall, except with the unanimous sanction of the meeting, be by show of hands and the chairman shall have a casting vote.

14. *Committee*.—At the first general meeting of the club, which shall be held in every year, one-fourth of the members of committee, or if their number be not a multiple of four, then the number nearest to one-fourth shall retire, and their places shall be filled up by the election of members of the club thereto.

15. The members of committee to retire in every year shall be those who have served longest on the committee, or in case of equal seniority they shall (in default of agreement among themselves), be selected by ballot. The retiring members shall be eligible for re-election at the election next succeeding to their retirement.

16. The committee may appoint sub-committees for any special purposes and may delegate to them such of the powers of the committee as they think fit.

17. The committee may make such regulations and bye-laws as they shall think fit for the conduct of the club or any of its prize meetings, shows or field trials, or otherwise in relation to the objects and purposes of the club, provided that no alteration may be made in these rules without the sanction of a general meeting.

18. Any member of the committee may at any time summon a meeting of the committee.

19. The members of the club may at any general meeting, by a resolution of which due notice shall have been given, and which shall be carried by a majority of not less than three-fourths of the

members of the club for the time being, remove any member of the committee, and they may elect in the usual manner another member to fill his place during such time as he would have held office if he had not been so removed.

20. *President.*—At the first general meeting of the club which shall be held in every year, a member of the club shall be elected to fill the office of president, and he shall hold office until the first general meeting of the club which shall be held in the year next succeeding his election. A retiring president shall be eligible for re-election at the election next succeeding his retirement.

21. The president of the club shall be chairman, and have a casting vote at all meetings of the committee and of all sub-committees on which he may serve.

22. Any casual vacancy occurring in the office of president or member of the committee may be filled up by the committee at any time by the election of a member of the club, who shall hold office during such time only as the person vacating the office would have held the same.

23. *Report, Audit, &c.*—All expenses incurred by the secretary or treasurer for or on behalf of the club shall be defrayed out of the funds of the club. An annual report, together with the rules of the club, the names of the members and officers, and the annual abstract of accounts (duly audited by two members), shall be printed and supplied to each member not later than the 31st of January in each year.

24. *Challenge Trophy.*—A grand challenge trophy shall be offered by the club for competition not less than twice nor oftener than four times in each year. It shall be a perpetual challenge trophy, and a piece of plate value £10 shall be given to any one who wins it three times, and the club's medal shall be given with the trophy each time it is offered for competition. The club's medal shall also be given each time the trophy is offered for competition to the breeder (if then known) of the dog or bitch who shall win the trophy, except when such breeder shall have already received a medal as exhibitor or as breeder of such dog or bitch, when the medal shall be withheld. No prizes or cups shall be offered for competition at shows not conforming to the Kennel Club Rules in every respect.

The Rules and Regulations of the Collie Club for Scotland, of which Mr. James E. McKillop, Dunfermline, is the secretary, and Mr. D. J. T. Gray, of Dundee, the president, are as follows:

1. *Name of Club and Objects.*—The name of the club shall be "The Scottish Collie Club," and its objects shall be to promote the breeding of pure collies, to define precisely, and publish a description of, the true type, and to urge the adoption of such type on breeders, judges, and dog show committees, as the only recognized standard by which collies are to be judged, and which may be accepted in future as the standard of excellence in breeding and judging, and by giving prizes, supporting shows, encouraging sheep dog trials, and by any other means, to do all in its power to protect and advance the interests of the breed.

2. *Qualification of Members.*—Admission to the membership is open to all who are favourable to the objects of the club.

3. *Election of Members.*—Persons wishing to become members must be proposed and seconded by two existing members, and the committee shall have full power to accept or refuse any newly proposed member.

4. *Subscription.*—The entrance fee on admission to the club shall be 10s. 6d., and the annual subscription 10s. 6d., payable by 1st January in each year. Any one failing to pay his subscription by the 31st March shall be liable to have his name struck off the list of members.

5. *Management of Club.*—Subject to the powers exerciseable by general meetings, the control and management of the club shall be vested in a committee of twelve members, a president and vice-presidents, secretary, and treasurer, to be elected from the general body of members—five to form a quorum. The president, vice-presidents, secretary, and treasurer shall be elected annually, but shall be eligible for re-election. Three members of committee, to be selected by ballot, must retire annually, and shall not be eligible for re-election for one year.

6. *General Meeting.*—A general meeting of the club shall be held at least once yearly at such place and time as the committee shall deem most convenient. No standing rule can be rescinded

or member expelled from the club except at general meetings. At all general or other meetings the president, failing whom, the vice-president, shall take the chair, and failing both, a chairman shall be elected from the meeting. The chairman shall in every case have a casting vote. At general meetings eight shall form a quorum.

A special meeting may be called at any time by the secretary on receiving a written request from ten members, stating the object of meeting.

7. *Powers of Committee.*—The committee shall have sole power to consider the expenditure and general management of the club, arranging shows, or field trials, appointment of judges, and giving of special prizes, and making conditions and bye-laws as they may think fit, always in accordance with the objects and purposes of the club.

The committee shall have power to form themselves into sub-committees for special purposes if they think fit.

If any member of committee shall be absent from three consecutive meetings of committee, without having furnished a satisfactory explanation, the committee shall have power to strike his name off the committee and fill up the vacancy.

8. *Withdrawal of Members.*—Any member wishing to withdraw from the club must intimate the same to the secretary in writing before 1st January in each year, otherwise he shall be held liable for the current year's subscription.

9. *Expulsion of Members.*—Any member violating the rules of the club, or who shall be proved to the satisfaction of the committee to have misconducted himself in any way in connection with dogs or dog shows, or shall have done anything not in accordance with legitimate exhibiting, shall be liable to be expelled from the club.

10. *Expenses.*—All expenses (including railway fares) incurred by the secretary and treasurer for or on behalf of the club shall be defrayed out of the funds of the club. An annual report of which (duly audited by two members) shall be published, together with the rules of the club and list of office-bearers, and supplied to each member.

## The Northern and Midland Sheep Dog Club.

QUITE recently another collie club has been formed, its establishment, judging from the early list of members, which already includes fifty-five names, being on a sound basis. Named the "Northern and Midland Sheep Dog Club," its objects are "the encouragement and improvement of the breed of sheep dogs by giving special prizes, supporting shows, publishing the description, urging the adoption of true type, and using every endeavour to advance the interests of the breed." Not a word about working the dogs, for which there is such a wide and useful field open. The "description" has not yet been published, but it can differ very little from that already given in this volume.

A special feature is made by an arrangement for breeders' challenge cups, value twenty-five guineas each—one for the best dog, another for the best bitch, bred by and exhibited by the same member of the club. These cups can only be won once by the same dog, but either trophy gained three times in all by the same member becomes his property.

There are two or three other novelties in the rules, and one of them determines that of the committee, twelve in number, six shall be members resident north of Derby, and six who reside south of the same place; three to form a quorum. Then the general meetings are to be movable, and, as occasion requires, will be held in Manchester, Birmingham, and Liverpool, or in any other town the committee may think desirable. Four such general meetings must be held annually.

An important rule is that one dealing with the selection

of judges, of which eight are to be elected annually by the votes of the general members of the club. No one but a member is open for nomination as a judge. It may be interesting to state that at the first election of this kind the following gentlemen were chosen to officiate for the year 1890-91, viz., Mr. L. C. P. Astley, Dudley; Mr. S. Boddington, Birmingham; Mr. Carpenter, Acock's Green, near Birmingham; Dr. McGill, Littleborough; Mr. A. H. Megson, Manchester; Mr. W. W. Steward, Rugby; Mr. T. H. Stretch, Ormskirk; and Mr. C. Wheeler, Birmingham.

The annual subscription is fixed at thirty shillings, with an entry fee of one guinea after the expiration of 1890, and life members can be made by the payment in one sum of ten guineas. The honorary secretary is Mr. H. Macbeth, Priory Bank, Sale, Cheshire.

*Advertisements.*

# BARNARD, BISHOP, AND BARNARDS
### LIMITED.

Manufacturers of every description of Appliance for the Kennel on most approved principles.

Illustrated Catalogue free by post.

"REGISTERED DESIGN."

### NEW
### Portable Dog Kennels.

No. 344. Finished in the best possible style, each house 4ft. square by 6ft. high to eaves by 7½ft. to ridge. Yards each 6ft. long by 4ft. wide, provided with Day Bench and Reversible Trough. They are well ventilated, and constructed on scientific principles, securing the maximum of comfort to our canine friends.

Price, complete, £15 10s.

If with corrugated iron at sides, as illustrated, 13s. 6d. extra.

### NEW ARTICLE.
### Improved Puppy Kennel.

No. 354. 6ft. long by 2ft. 6in. wide, by 2ft. 6in. high.

Price, complete with reversible trough, £2 10s.

Testimonial from S. Cooper, Esq., Fairlawn, Haywards Heath.—"The house I bought of you for a puppy run I have hitherto used as a chicken run, and find it answers admirably for that purpose, and I like it much."

"REGISTERED DESIGN."

### Improved Dog's Kennel.

No. 348. For Terriers, 20s. each.

No. 349. For Retrievers and Colleys, 35s. each.

No. 350. For Mastiffs and St. Bernards, 55s. each.

If with lifting front, as shewn in illustration, to form a shelter from sun and rain, 2s. 6d., 3s., and 4s. each extra respectively.

Draw out Day Benches, 5s., 7s. 6d., and 10s. 6d. each extra respectively.

Ornamental Dog Railing, No. 383, 5ft. high, at 6s. 6d. per yard; Gates and Locks, 20s. 6d.
,,   ,,   ,,   ,,   6ft.  ,,   ,, 7s. 6d.   ,,   ,,   ,,   22s. 6d.
,,   ,,   ,,   ,,   7ft.  ,,   ,, 8s. 6d.   ,,   ,,   ,,   25s. 6d.

## Manufactory: Norfolk Iron Works, Norwich.
## London Show Rooms: 91-95, QUEEN VICTORIA STREET, E.C.

*Advertisements.*

Under Royal Patronage at Home and Abroad.
## MANGE, SURFEIT, ERUPTIONS, BLOTCH, LOSS OF COAT, AND ALL SKIN DISEASES.
### DOGS, HORSES, AND OTHER ANIMALS.
# Elias Bishop's Celebrated Lotion,
## OGWELL, NEWTON ABBOT.

Perfectly Free from Poison, Oils, or Grease. The Lotion destroys all Lice, Fleas, or Ticks. Hundreds of Testimonials of Cases cured when all other remedies had failed. Forwarded to any part of the World in *Tin Cans*, 1 Quart, 2s. 6d., *Parcel Post*, 3s.; 2 Quarts, 4s. 6d., *Parcel Post*, 5s. 6d.; 1 Gallon, 8s.; 2 Gallons, 15s. Can be obtained through all Chemists—of Messrs. Barclay and Sons, 95, Farringdon Street; Messrs. W. Edwards and Sons, 239, Upper Thames Street; Messrs. Sanger and Sons, 150 and 252, Oxford Street, London; and of Messrs. Raimes, Blanchards, and Co., Edinburgh.

### Extract from the "Field:"

BISHOP'S MANGE LOTION.—We have received several letters from gentlemen who have tried this Lotion with an excellent result, in consequence of our recommendation to that effect. From their account, which may be taken as reliable, since they are all experienced in canine matters, the Lotion is a great boon to owners of dogs. Mr. Bishop's address is Ogwell, Newton Abbot.

Mr. Lort says: "I have given the Lotion a good trial, and like it."

Mr. Whitehouse says: "It has proved successful in every case; is invaluable for skin diseases."

Mr. J. H. Salter says: "Being non-poisonous, I have dressed bitches with puppies on them; cured the mother without damage to the offspring."

The Rev. Cumming Macdona says: "There is nothing that will prevent and cure mange and all skin diseases like Elias Bishop's Lotion."

The Rev. W. Sergeantson says: "The Lotion is most effective, easily applied, free from grease and smell."

Rev. W. J. Mellor says: "I consider your Lotion an excellent remedy for red mange and blotch; only had occasion to use it twice; both cases it effected a perfect cure in a very short time."

Mr. T. Webber says: "Your Lotion has cured my dogs, and I most strongly recommend it to every sportsman."

Mr. W. D. Duncan says: "Elias Bishop's Mange Lotion. I have found it the best remedy I have ever tried, and that out of a good many. If the heat which he sees is treated with it in time, he will have little trouble in soon making it disappear, but even in very bad cases I have never found it fail. I first tried it on a mare that was very bad, and my V.S. could do nothing for her; that is, everything he tried failed. I told him I had Bishop's Lotion, and I tried it on one side; he went on with his treatment on the other side of her. In a week my side was nearly well, and his not one bit better; so we then used it on both sides, and in a short time she was all right, and has never been troubled with it again, whereas before that every spring she used to break out with it. With dogs I never have any cases bad, as I always take it in time, and I feel sure if J. C. has not tried it he will soon have his kennel all right if he will use the Lotion; there is very little trouble with it."

Mr. Edgar Hanbury says: "I have just made the most successful cure I have ever taken in hand by the use of your valuable Lotion, in the case of a mastiff bitch, which came to me some months ago sadly infected with mange; so badly, in fact, that I once thought it was almost hopeless; but, by following *all* your directions to the *letter* and paying great attention to her diet, &c., she is now perfectly recovered, and her coat is like silk, and I have every reason to think that she will not be troubled with it again. I could mention many other instances of *obstinate* mange where I have met with the same result, but the above is decidedly the worst that I have ever come across, and proves the wonderful power of your mixture. Pray make use of these remarks in any way you like."

Miss M. Norton says: "Some time ago you sent me a quart of your Lotion to put on our little black and tan terrier. I am very glad to say it has quite cured him, and instead of him having hardly any coat, he has now got a thick glossy one. Our vet. here told us that the dog could not be cured, and that we had better kill him; he described the disease as 'eczema.' We shall always recommend your Lotion with great pleasure, again thanking you very much."

Mr. Vero Shaw says: "I have tried the Mange Lotion I had from you the other day, and it has acted like magic upon a couple of greyhounds which had mange badly, and upon which a number of the usual remedies had had no effect. As long as I keep dogs I never shall be without some of your Mange Lotion on the premises, and shall recommend it to my friends. You are quite at liberty to make any use you like of this."

# 1890.

## A Catalogue of Books

RELATING TO

Angling, Boating, Cricket, Farming, Gardening, Hunting, Shooting, Tennis, Travel, Yachting, &c.,

USEFUL FOR

## COUNTRY GENTLEMEN,
### TRAVELLERS, ETC.,

*PUBLISHED BY*

## HORACE COX,

"THE FIELD" OFFICE, 346, STRAND, LONDON, W.C.

---

*\*\** *Orders for any of the following works, with postage stamps or post-office order (payable at the Money Order Office, 369, Strand) for the amount, should be sent to* HORACE COX, *Publisher, at the above address, or they may be obtained by order of any bookseller.*

# NOTE.

I BEG to call the attention of Country Gentlemen, Travellers, Sportsmen, Farmers, and others to the works quoted in this Catalogue. They are written by authors who are well known and acknowledged authorities on their respective subjects.

The illustrations have been intrusted to competent artists, and neither pains nor expense have been spared to make the works as complete as possible.

HORACE COX,<br>Publisher.

# A CATALOGUE OF BOOKS

PUBLISHED BY

## HORACE COX.

---

**SECOND EDITION, GREATLY ENLARGED.**

*Royal 4to., bevelled boards, gilt edges, price 15s., by post 15s. 9d.*

# PHEASANTS:
### THEIR
# NATURAL HISTORY AND PRACTICAL MANAGEMENT.

By W. B. TEGETMEIER, F.Z.S.,
(*Member of the British Ornithologists' Union.*)
AUTHOR OF "THE NATURAL HISTORY OF THE CRANES," &c., &c.

Illustrated with numerous full-page engravings drawn from Life by
T. W. WOOD.

---

Great Reduction in Price of DAY'S BRITISH AND IRISH FISHES.

*In 2 vols., imperial 8vo., cloth, price 3 guineas. Published originally at 5 guineas.* THE

# FISHES OF GREAT BRITAIN AND IRELAND.

By FRANCIS DAY, F.L.S., F.Z.S., &c.

Mr. HORACE COX begs to announce that he has purchased the Copyright of this valuable Standard Work, and has very much reduced the price, in order to render it more easily available to Students of Natural History.

This work contains nearly TWO HUNDRED PLATES, and many Woodcuts.

---

Greatly Reduced in Price. DAY'S SALMONIDÆ.

*In 1 vol., imperial 8vo., cloth, price 1 guinea. Published at 2 guineas.
With 12 Coloured Plates and many Woodcuts.*

# British and Irish Salmonidæ.

By FRANCIS DAY, C.I.E, F.L.S., AND F.Z.S.

This work is an exhaustive treatise on the Salmonidæ of the British Islands and will be interesting to the Fisherman, as well as a text-book to the Scientific Ichthyologist. The reduced price will place it within the reach of all.

A Few Copies to be had, beautifully bound in Whole Calf, Full Gilt, price 35s.

---

"THE FIELD" OFFICE, 346, STRAND, W.C.

A CATALOGUE OF BOOKS.

*Price 2s. 6d., by post 2s. 10d.*

# THE
# YACHT RACING CALENDAR
# AND REVIEW.

BY

## DIXON KEMP, A.I.N.A.,

Author of "Yacht and Boat Sailing," &c.

**CONTENTS:**

CALENDAR OF RACES SAILED.
TABULAR ABSTRACT OF MATCHES SAILED.
TABLE OF WINNING YACHTS.
PROTESTS.
REVIEW OF YACHT RACING, 1889.
GENERAL REVIEW.
BOOKS FOR YACHTSMEN.
MEETING OF THE YACHT RACING ASSOCIATION.
YACHT RACING RULES AND REGULATIONS.
Y.R.A. CERTIFICATES OF RATING.
LOGS OF CRUISES.
MISCELLANEOUS EVENTS AND NOTICES.
PARAGRAPH NOTICES.
LAUNCHES AND TRIAL TRIPS.
NOTES OF INFORMATION (Illustrated).
OBITUARY.
ILLUSTRATED ARTICLES.
CANOEING.

"THE FIELD" OFFICE, 346, STRAND, W.C.

PUBLISHED BY HORACE COX.

## SIXTH EDITION.

*Super-royal 8vo., price 25s., or by post 26s.*

# A MANUAL
## OF
# YACHT AND BOAT SAILING.

### By DIXON KEMP,
Associate Institute Naval Architects (Member of the Council).

AUTHOR OF "YACHT DESIGNING" AND "YACHT ARCHITECTURE."

(The Lords Commissioners of the Admiralty have ordered this work to be supplied to the Libraries of the ships of the Royal Navy.)

This Edition has been largely re-written, and contains a great number of new subjects, and the lines of many boats never before published, the total number of Plates exceeding 100, besides more than 350 woodcuts in the text.

### CONTENTS.

CHAP.
- I.—Selecting a Yacht.
- II.—Examination and Survey of the Yacht before Purchasing.
- III.—Building a Yacht.
- IV.—The Equipment of the Yacht.
- V.—Seamanship.
- VI.—The Management of Open Boats.
- VII.—The General Management of a Yacht.
- VIII.—Yacht Racing.
- IX.—Handling a Yacht in a Match.
- X.—Centre-Boards.
- XI.—Centre-Board Boats for Rowing and Sailing.
- XII.—Sails for Centre-Board Boats.
- XIII.—Small Centre-Board Yachts.
- XIV.—Mersey Sailing Boats.

CHAP.
- XV.—Clyde Sailing Boats.
- XVI.—Belfast Lough Boats.
- XVII.—Kingstown Boats.
- XVIII.—Cork Harbour Boats.
- XIX.—Itchen Boats.
- XX.—Falmouth Quay Punts.
- XXI.—Thames Bawley Boats.
- XXII.—Windermere Yachts.
- XXIII.—Yachts of the Norfolk Broads.
- XXIV.—Yachts of 3 Tons, 5 Rating, and 2½ Rating.
- XXV.—Single-Handed Cruisers.
- XXVI.—Types of Sailing Vessels.
- XXVII.—Double Boats.
- XXVIII.—Steam Yachting.
- XXIX.—Ice Yachting.
- XXX.—Canoeing.

APPENDIX contains complete instructions as to Practical Boat Building. This section is arranged alphabetically in the form of a dictionary, and embodies a variety of information connected with Yachts, Boats, the customs of the sea, laws relating to seamen, nautical terms, and in fact everything which might be expected in a nautical cyclopædia.

*Full instruction is given as to the building and management of every boat described.*

"THE FIELD" OFFICE, 346, STRAND, W.C.

ILLUSTRATED WITH FULL-PAGE ENGRAVINGS DRAWN PRINCIPALLY FROM LIFE BY HARRISON WEIR.

*In Imperial 4to., bevelled boards, gilt edges, price 18s., by post 18s. 9d.*

# THE CATTLE OF GREAT BRITAIN:
## BEING A SERIES OF ARTICLES
ON THE
VARIOUS BREEDS OF CATTLE OF THE UNITED KINGDOM, THEIR HISTORY, MANAGEMENT, &c.

Edited by the late J. COLEMAN,

Editor of the Farm Department of "The Field," and formerly Professor of Agriculture at the Royal Agricultural College, Cirencester.

---

ILLUSTRATED WITH FULL-PAGE ENGRAVINGS DRAWN PRINCIPALLY FROM LIFE BY HARRISON WEIR.

*In Imperial 4to., bevelled boards, gilt edges, price 18s., by post 18s. 9d.*

# THE SHEEP AND PIGS OF GREAT BRITAIN:
## BEING A SERIES OF ARTICLES
ON THE VARIOUS
BREEDS OF SHEEP AND PIGS OF THE UNITED KINGDOM, THEIR HISTORY MANAGEMENT, &c.

Edited by the late J. COLEMAN,

Editor of the Farm Department of "The Field," and formerly Professor of Agriculture at the Royal Agricultural College, Cirencester.

---

THIRD EDITION (REVISED 1889). *Price 7s. 6d., by post 7s. 10d.*

# A SYSTEM OF FIGURE SKATING.
BY
H. E. VANDERVELL AND T. MAXWELL WITHAM
(MEMBERS OF THE SKATING CLUB).

The present Revised Edition contains a New Chapter describing the Club Figures, which will enable country skaters to perfect themselves in the art of combined skating.

---

FOURTH EDITION. *In post 8vo., limp cloth, gilt, price 2s. 6d., by post 2s. 8d.*

# THE ART OF SKATING;
WITH
ILLUSTRATIONS, DIAGRAMS, AND PLAIN DIRECTIONS FOR THE ACQUIREMENT OF THE MOST DIFFICULT AND GRACEFUL MOVEMENTS.

By GEORGE ANDERSON ("Cyclos"),

Vice-President of the Crystal Palace Skating Club, and for many years President of the Glasgow Skating Club.

---

"THE FIELD" OFFICE, 346, STRAND, W.C.

PUBLISHED BY HORACE COX. 7

NEW AND CHEAPER EDITION OF THE CATTLE, SHEEP, AND PIGS OF GREAT BRITAIN.
*With Illustrations from the original drawings by Harrison Weir, in 1 vol., price 12s. 6d., by post 13s.*

# THE
# CATTLE, SHEEP, AND PIGS
## OF
# GREAT BRITAIN:
### BEING
## A SERIES OF ARTICLES
#### ON THE VARIOUS
### BREEDS OF THE UNITED KINGDOM, THEIR HISTORY, MANAGEMENT, &c.

Edited by the late JOHN COLEMAN,
Editor of the Farm Department of "The Field," and formerly Professor of Agriculture at the R y Agricultural College, Cirencester.

## CONTENTS.

### THE CATTLE OF GREAT BRITAIN.

I. Introductory.
II. Breeding and General Management.
III. Principles of Feeding and Value of Different Kinds of Food.
IV. Buildings and the Management of Manure.
V. Dairy Management, the Milk Trade, &c.
VI. Shorthorns. By John Thornton.
VII. The Hereford Breed of Cattle. By T. Duckham.
VIII. Devon Breed of Cattle. By Lieut.-Col. J. T. Davy.
IX. The Longhorns. By Gilbert Murray.
X. The Sussex Breed of Cattle. By A. Heasman.
XI. Norfolk and Suffolk Red-Polled Cattle. By Thomas Fulcher.
XII. Galloway Cattle. By Gilbert Murray.
XIII. The Angus-Aberdeen Cattle.
XIV. The Ayrshire Breed of Cattle. By Gilbert Murray.
XV. West Highland Cattle. By John Robertson.
XVI. The Glamorgan Breed of Cattle. By Morgan Evans.
XVII. Pembrokeshire or Castlemartin Cattle. By Morgan Evans.
XVIII. The Anglesea Cattle. By Morgan Evans.
XIX. The Kerry Breed of Cattle. By the late R. O. Pringle.
XX. The Jersey Breed of Cattle. By John M. Hall.
XXI. The Guernsey Breed of Cattle. By "A Native."

### THE SHEEP OF GREAT BRITAIN.

I. Introductory.
II. The Management of Ewes up to Lambing.
III. Preparations for and Attention during Lambing.
IV. Management from Birth to Weaning.
V. From Weaning to Market.
VI. On Wool.
VII. Leicester Sheep.
VIII. Border Leicesters. By John Usher.
IX. Cotswold Sheep.
X. Long-Woolled Lincoln Sheep.
XI. The Devon Long-Wools. By Joseph Darby.
XII. Romney Marsh Sheep.
XIII. Southdown Sheep.
XIV. The Hampshire or West Country Down Sheep. By E. P. Squarey.
XV. Shropshire Sheep.
XVI. Oxfordshire Down Sheep. By Messrs. A. F. M. Druce and C. Hobbs.
XVII. The Roscommon Sheep. By he late R. O. Pringle.
XVIII. Negrette Merino Sheep.
XIX. Exmoor Sheep.
XX. The Black-faced or Scotch Mountain Sheep.
XXI. Cheviot Sheep. By John Usher.
XXII. Dorset Horned Sheep. By Joseph Darby.
XXIII. Welsh Mountain Sheep. By Morgan Evans.
XXIV. The Radnor Sheep. By Morgan Evans.
XXV. Herdwick Sheep. By H. A. Spedding.

### THE PIGS OF GREAT BRITAIN.

I. Introductory.
II. The Berkshire Pig.
III. Black Suffolk Pigs.
IV. Large White Breed of Pigs.
V. Small White Pigs.
VI. Middle Bred White Pigs.
VII. The Black Dorset Pig.
VIII. The Tamworth Pig.

"THE FIELD" OFFICE, 346, STRAND, W.C.

## FIFTH EDITION.

*Re-written, with additions and new full-page engravings. In one volume, bevelled boards, gilt edges, price 15s. by post 15s. 9d.*

THE

# Dogs of the British Islands:

BEING

## A SERIES OF ARTICLES

ON

## THE POINTS OF THEIR VARIOUS BREEDS,

AND

## THE TREATMENT OF THE DISEASES TO WHICH THEY ARE SUBJECT.

REPRINTED FROM "THE FIELD" NEWSPAPER.

### By the late J. H. WALSH,
"STONEHENGE," EDITOR OF "THE FIELD."
(WITH THE AID OF SEVERAL EXPERIENCED BREEDERS.)

---

### CONTENTS.

#### GENERAL MANAGEMENT.

Book
I.—Management of Dogs in Health.
II.—Drugs Commonly Used for the Diseases of Dogs, and their Modes of Administration.

Book
III.—The Ordinary Diseases of the Dog and their Treatment.
IV.—Judging at Dog Shows and Field Trials.

#### SPORTING DOGS.

Book
I.—Dogs Used with the Gun.

Book
II.—Hounds and their Allies.

#### NON-SPORTING DOGS.

Book
I.—Watch Dogs.
II.—Sheep and Cattle Dogs.

Book
III.—Terriers (other than Fox and Toy).
IV.—Toy Dogs.

---

SECOND EDITION. *Large post 8vo., price 7s. 6d., by post 8s.*

THE

# "IDSTONE" PAPERS.

## A SERIES OF ARTICLES AND DESULTORY OBSERVATIONS ON SPORT AND THINGS IN GENERAL.

BY

### "IDSTONE,"
OF "THE FIELD."

---

"THE FIELD" OFFICE, 346, STRAND, W.C.

PUBLISHED BY HORACE COX.

**PUBLISHED ANNUALLY.**
Vol. III., 1889-90, *price* 2s. 6d., *by post* 2s. 10d.

THE

# GOLFING ANNUAL.

### EDITED BY D. S. DUNCAN.

*\*\*\** The attention of golfers is called to this work, which differs from kindred publications in many respects. It contains Original Articles, not merely Reprints; and its Club Directory is the only Complete and Accurate List of Golf Clubs and Description of Golf Greens ever published.

**THIS WORK CONTAINS ABOVE 700 PAGES, AND NEARLY 400 ILLUSTRATIONS.**

*Second Edition, with additions, price* 25s., *by post* 26s., *cloth gilt.*

# Shifts and Expedients

OF

## CAMP LIFE, TRAVEL, AND EXPLORATION.

BY

### W. B. LORD and T. BAINES.
(Royal Artillery.)   (F.R.G.S.)

### CONTENTS.

INTRODUCTION.
Chap.
- I.—Outfit to take abroad.
- II.—Boats, Rafts, and Makeshift Floats.
- III.—Working in Metal.
- IV.—Huts and Houses.
- V.—Extempore Bridges and Makeshifts for Crossing Rivers and Ravines.
- VI.—Timber and its Utilisation.
- VII.—Sledges and Sledge Travelling.
- VIII.—Boots, Shoes, and Sandals.
- IX.—Waggons and other Wheeled Vehicles.
- X.—Harness and Pack Animals.
- XI.—Camels.
- XII.—Cattle Marking.
- XIII.—Water, and the Sap of Plants.
- XIV.—Camp Cookery.

Chap.
- XV.—Fish and Amphibious Animals.
- XVI.—Poisoned Weapons, Arrows, Spears, &c.
- XVII.—Tracking, Hunting, and Trapping.
- XVIII.—Palanquins, Stretchers, Ambulances, &c.
- XIX.—On Sketching and Painting under the Ordinary Difficulties of Travel.
- XX.—The Estimation of Distances and Hints on Field Observing.
- XXI.—Hints to Explorers on Collecting and Preserving Objects of Natural History.
- XXII.—Ropes and Twines.
- XXIII.—Bush Veterinary Surgery and Medicine.

"THE FIELD" OFFICE, 346, STRAND, W.C.

*Second Edition, demy 8vo., printed on plate paper, with Illustrations on toned paper, price 3s. 6d., by post 3s. 11d.,*

A HISTORY AND DESCRIPTION, WITH REMINISCENCES, OF

# THE FOX TERRIER.

By RAWDON B. LEE,
*Kennel Editor of "The Field."*

THE ILLUSTRATIONS BY ARTHUR WARDLE.

**A FEW COPIES ON LARGE PAPER, Price 10s. 6d., by Post 11s.**

*Now ready, demy 8vo., printed on plate paper, with Illustrations by Arthur Wardle, price 3s. 6d., by post 3s. 11d.*

A HISTORY AND DESCRIPTION
OF THE

# COLLIE OR SHEEP DOG,

IN HIS BRITISH VARIETIES.

By RAWDON B. LEE,
*Kennel Editor of "The Field," and Author of "The Fox Terrier."*

**A FEW COPIES ON LARGE PAPER, Price 10s. 6d., by Post 11s.**

*Demy 8vo., pp. 480, price 15s., by post 16s.,* VOLUME I. of
THE

# MODERN SPORTSMAN'S GUN AND RIFLE,

INCLUDING

GAME AND WILDFOWL GUNS, SPORTING AND MATCH RIFLES, AND REVOLVERS.

IN TWO VOLUMES.

Vol. I.—GAME AND WILDFOWL GUNS.

BY THE LATE J. H. WALSH,
"STONEHENGE," EDITOR OF "THE FIELD,"
Author of "Dogs of the British Islands," "The Greyhound," "British Rural Sports," &c.

"THE FIELD" OFFICE, 346, STRAND, W.C.

PUBLISHED BY HORACE COX. 11

*Demy 8vo., pp.* 500, *with* 200 *Illustrations, price* 15s.,
*by post* 16s., VOLUME II. *of*

THE
# MODERN SPORTSMAN'S GUN AND RIFLE,
INCLUDING
## GAME AND WILDFOWL GUNS, SPORTING AND MATCH RIFLES, AND REVOLVERS.

Vol. II.—THE RIFLE AND REVOLVER.

BY THE LATE J. H. WALSH,
"STONEHENGE," EDITOR OF "THE FIELD,"
*Author of "Dogs of the British Islands," "The Greyhound," "British Rural Sports," &c.*

**CONTENTS.**

Definitions, &c.—Theory of Projectiles—The Mechanical Construction of the Sporting Rifle and its Ammunition—Modern Rifled Pistols—The Match or Target Rifle and its Ammunition.

*Demy 4to., with 12 full-page illustrations, some of which contain Portraits of Sporting Celebrities, and 24 vignettes, price £1 1s., by post £1 2s.*

# SPORTING SKETCHES
WITH
## PEN AND PENCIL.

BY THE LATE
### FRANCIS FRANCIS AND A. W. COOPER.

**CONTENTS.**

The First of September.
A Day in a Punt.
Mark Cock!
Trouting.
Long Tails and Short Ones.
Paying the Pike.

Rabbit Shooting.
Roaching.
Grouse Shooting.
Salmon Fishing.
Snipe Shooting.
Grayling Fishing.

"THE FIELD" OFFICE, 346, STRAND, W.C.

## A PRESENTATION VOLUME FOR CLUBS.

4to., bevelled boards, gilt edges (500 pages), with appropriate illustrations, price One Guinea, by post £1 2s. 4d.

THE

# ENGLISH GAME OF CRICKET:

COMPRISING A DIGEST OF ITS

## ORIGIN, CHARACTER, HISTORY, AND PROGRESS,

TOGETHER WITH

## AN EXPOSITION OF ITS LAWS AND LANGUAGE.

BY

## CHARLES BOX,

Author of "The Cricketers' Manual," "Reminiscences of Celebrated Players," Essays on the Game, "Songs and Poems," "Theory and Practice of Cricket," &c.

### CONTENTS.

Chap.
I. to VI.} Introductory.

**GLANCES AT THE PAST AND PRESENT STATE OF COUNTY CRICKET.**

VII.—Middlesex.
VIII.—Public School Matches.
IX.—Kent.
X.—Hampshire.
XI.—Surrey.
XII.—Sussex.
XIII.—Nottinghamshire.
XIV.—Yorkshire.

Chap.
XV.—Warwickshire and Derbyshire.
XVI.—Gloucestershire.
XVII.—Lancashire and Leicestershire.
XVIII.—The Eastern Counties.
XIX. XX.} Intercolonial Matches.
XXI.—School and Village Matches.
XXII.—Curiosities of Cricket.
XXIII.—Cricket Grounds.
XXIV.—Laws of the Game.
XXV.—Poems, Songs, and Ballads.
XXVI.—Glossary of Words and Phrases.
POSTSCRIPT.—Shakespeare and Cricket —An Enforced Dissertation.

### OPINIONS OF THE PRESS.

"The most complete and interesting work on cricket ever published. No expense has been spared in making that which is really useful a very handsome volume."—*Bell's Life.*

"We welcome with heartiness a writer like Mr. Charles Box, who has so pleasantly united in the splendid volume before us the old order (of cricket) with the new."—*Sporting and Dramatic News.*

"This work will prove interesting to all lovers of cricket."—*Times.*

"The volume is a very handsome one indeed, destined, doubtless, to become an authority on the essentially 'English Game of Cricket.'"—*Morning Post.*

"The best work on cricket that has yet come under our notice."—*Nottingham Journal.*

"A handsome and well got-up volume, the author being the man of all others qualified and in a position for compiling such a work."—*Kent Herald.*

"THE FIELD" OFFICE, 346, STRAND, W.C.

*Crown 4to., printed on toned paper, price 15s., by post 16s.*

# THE ANNALS OF TENNIS.

### BY
### JULIAN MARSHALL.

This work will be found very complete, and, it is thought, justly entitled to take its place as the standard work on Tennis. It has cost its author much laborious research; and, independently of its great value to tennis players and all lovers of the game, it is trusted, from the vast amount of curious lore it contains, the volume will be found not unworthy of a place on the shelves of the scholar. The author, himself a well-known amateur, is fully competent to speak with authority on the game, having had the opportunity of studying the play of the best Continental, in addition to that of the best English, masters, and, therefore, may be taken as a safe guide by learners.

### CONTENTS.

I.—Tennis Abroad.
II.—Tennis in England.
III.—The Court and Implements.
IV.—The Laws and their History.
V.—The Game.
VI.—Appendix.

---

*Second Edition. Large post 8vo., price 5s., by post 5s. 3d.*

# ANGLING.

### BY THE LATE
### FRANCIS FRANCIS.

*Author of "A Book on Angling," "By Lake and River," "Hot Pot," &c.*

### CONTENTS.

Preface.
Chap.
I.—The Art of Angling.
II.—Mid-Water Fishing.
III.—Surface or Fly Fishing.
IV.—The Gudgeon, the Pope or Ruff, the Bleak, the Roach, the Rudd, the Dace, the Chub, the Barbel, the Bream, the Carp, the Tench, the Perch.

Chap.
V.—The Pike.
VI.—Trout Fishing with Bait.
VII.—Fly Fishing for Trout.
VIII.—Trout Flies.
IX.—Grayling Fishing.
X.—Salmon Fishing.
XI.—Salmon Flies.
XII.—On Tackle Making.
Addenda.

---

*Post 8vo., in cloth, price 5s., by post 5s. 4d.*

# HOT-POT.
## MISCELLANEOUS PAPERS
### BY THE LATE
### FRANCIS FRANCIS,

*Author of "A Book on Angling," "By Lake and River," "Angling," &c.*

"THE FIELD" OFFICE, 346, STRAND, W.C.

*Crown 8vo., price 1s., by post 1s. 2d., in Coloured Wrapper, and Page Illustrations drawn by* WHYMPER.

# TWENTY-SIX YEARS' REMINISCENCES

OF

# SCOTCH GROUSE MOORS.

## By W. A. ADAMS.

**CONTENTS.**

Seasons 1863 to 1888—A Hare Day—Remarks on the Outcome of Disease—Heather-Burning and Draining—Surface Draining—Dogs—Disease—Wildfowl—Conclusion—Summary.

*Demy 8vo., with folding plates and full-page illustrations printed on toned paper, price 21s., by post 21s. 9d.*

# MODERN WILDFOWLING.

BY

## LEWIS CLEMENT,

"WILDFOWLER."

OPINIONS OF THE PRESS.

"An excellent work indeed, and full of capital illustrations, is 'Modern Wildfowling;' to recommend it aright I should have, if I were clever enough, and it did not already exist, to invent the famous phrase, 'a book no gentleman's library should be without.'"—*Truth*, March 17, 1881.

"This book deals not only with the various modes of approaching, or decoying, and killing wildfowl of all kinds, but enters into minute details upon the construction of punts, both single and double handed; sails; punt guns, muzzle-loading as well as breechloading; recoil apparatus; and shoulder guns of all patterns, with the varying loads required for different bores. In addition to this are several chapters devoted to a narration of the adventures of the author while in pursuit of wildfowl, both at home and abroad—which are very pleasant reading. . . . . With the addition of a good index, sportsmen will have in this work a capital *vade mecum* on the art of wildfowling."—*The Zoologist* for November, 1880.

"THE FIELD" OFFICE, 346, STRAND, W.C.

PUBLISHED BY HORACE COX. 15

*Large post 8vo., price 3s. 6d., by post 3s. 9d.*

# PRACTICAL PHEASANT REARING:

WITH

## AN APPENDIX ON GROUSE DRIVING.

### By RICHARD JOHN LLOYD PRICE.

Author of "Rabbits for Profit and Rabbits for Powder," &c.

CONTENTS.

CHAP.
- I.—The General History of the Pheasant — Treating of the Pheasant and its Egg.
- II.—The Barn Door Hens.
- III.—The Eggs and the Appliances necessary for Hatching.
- IV.—Hatching Out—The Incubator.
- V.—The Rearing Field—Protection from Vermin.
- VI.—Moving of the Coops and Treatment of the Young Birds.

CHAP.
- VII.—Recipes for the Preparation of and Instructions for the proper Administration of the Food to Young Pheasants.
- VIII.—The Diseases of Young Pheasants and their Cure.
- IX.—Catching up, Moving into Coverts, and the proper Food for Older Birds.
- X.—Miscellaneous Remarks, and a few Words on Turkeys.

APPENDIX.

HINTS ON GROUSE DRIVING.

CHAP.
- I.—Practical Hints on Driving Grouse.
- II.—Practical Hints on Driving Grouse (continued).

CHAP.
- III.—The Working of the Drive, and the Duties of the Drivers.

*Large post 8vo., price 6s. 6d., by post 6s. 10d.*

# SKETCHES

OF

# LIFE, SCENERY, and SPORT

IN

# NORWAY.

BY

### Rev. M. R. BARNARD, B.A.,

Author of "Sport in Norway and Where to Find It," "Life of Thorvaldsen," and Translator of "Private Life of the Old Northmen," and a "Summer in Iceland," &c.

This work is admirably adapted for use as a Sporting Tourist's Handbook, while it is of absorbing interest to the general reader.

"THE FIELD" OFFICE, 346, STRAND, W.C.

*8vo. pp. 463, with 32 illustrations, price 16s., by post 16s. 10d.*

# ESSAYS
## ON
# SPORT AND NATURAL HISTORY.
### By J. E. HARTING.

**CONTENTS.**

Shooting—Hawking—Fishing—Training Hawks—Lark Mirrors—Plover Catching—Fishing with Cormorants—Decoys—The Irish Wolfhound—The Badger—Wild Turkeys—The Great Bustard—Seals—Wild Swans, &c.

Thirty-eight Essays: concluding with Practical Hints on Bird Preserving for the use of Travellers and Collectors.

---

*In demy 8vo., price 3s. 6d., by post 3s. 9d.*

# HINTS
## ON
# THE MANAGEMENT OF HAWKS,
### BY J. E. HARTING,
*Author of "A Handbook of British Birds," "Essays on Sport and Natural History."*

---

*Large post 8vo., price 6s., by post 6s. 4d.*

# RAMBLES AFTER SPORT;
## OR,
### TRAVELS AND ADVENTURES IN THE AMERICAS AND AT HOME.
#### BY
# "OLIVER NORTH."

**CONTENTS.**

A Week's Duck Shooting at Poole—That Sheldrake—Quail Shooting in California—Bear Hunting in Mexico—Bear Shooting in California—My First Elk—My Last Bear—Round Cape Horn, Valparaiso, Santiago—Andacollo, Lima, Panama, Jamaica—Country Sports and Life in Chile—Shooting in Chile—Two Days' Fishing in Chile—"Toling" for Ducks in California—Up the Sacramento—The White Elk of Astoria—Sport in the Coast Range Mountains.

---

*In large post 8vo., limp cloth, price 2s. 6d., by post 2s. 8d.*

# COLORADO:
## ITS
### AGRICULTURE, STOCKFEEDING, SCENERY, AND SHOOTING.
#### BY
### S. NUGENT TOWNSHEND, J.P.
("ST. KAMES.")

---

*Demy 8vo., price 1s., by post, 1s. 1d.*

## THE
# EARLY MATURITY OF LIVE STOCK.
### BY HENRY EVERSHED,
*Writer on Agriculture in the "Journal of the Royal Agricultural Society of England," "The Field," "Quarterly Review," &c.*

---

"THE FIELD" OFFICE, 346, STRAND, W.C.

VOLUMES I. and II. (containing Parts I. to VI.), in crown 8vo., red cloth, price 6s., by post 6s. 6d., each vol.

# THE
# HUNTING COUNTRIES
## OF
# ENGLAND,
## THEIR FACILITIES, CHARACTER, AND REQUIREMENTS.
## A GUIDE TO HUNTING MEN.
## BY "BROOKSBY."

### CONTENTS.

#### PART I.

Introduction.
The Belvoir.
The South Wold.

The Brocklesby.
The Burton and The Blankney.
The Fitzwilliam.
The Quorn.

The Cottesmore.
The Puckeridge.
The Old Berkeley.

#### PART II.

The North Warwickshire.
The Pytchley.
The Woodland Pytchley.
The Atherstone.
The Billesdon or South Quorn.
The Meynell. [Hunt.
The Bicester and Warden Hill

The Heythrop.
The Old Berkshire.
The South Oxfordshire.
The South Nottinghamshire.
The East Kent.
The Tickham.
The Vine.

The South Berkshire.
Mr. Garth's.
The H. H.
The Tedworth.
Lord Ferrers'.
The Warwickshire.

#### PART III.

The Dulverton.
The Stars of the West.
Mr. Luttrell's.
Lord Portsmouth's.
The Essex and the Essex Union.
The Hertfordshire.
The Whaddon Chase.

The Vale of White Horse.
The Cheshire and South Cheshire.
The Blackmoor Vale.
The Cambridgeshire.
The Duke of Grafton's.
The Holderness.

The Oakley.
The North Herefordshire.
The Duke of Buccleuch's.
The Tynedale.
Lord Percy's.
The Morpeth.
The Rufford.

### Also (VOLUME II.)

#### PART IV.

The Badsworth.
The Southdown.
The West Essex.
The Bramham Moor.
The East Sussex.
The Essex and Suffolk.
The York and Ainsty.

Lord Fitzwilliam's.
The Crawley and Horsham.
The West Kent.
Sir Watkin Wynn's.
The Hursley.
The Hambledon.
Lord Coventry's.

The Grove.
The West Norfolk.
The Bedale.
Lord Zetland's.
The Craven.
The Surrey Union.

#### PART V.

The Old Surrey.
Mr. Richard Combe's.
The Burstow.
The Hurworth.
The Cattistock.
The Suffolk.
The Shropshire.

The Earl of Radnor's.
Capt. Hon. F. Johnstone's.
The South Durham.
The Worcestershire.
The Ledbury.
The South Herefordshire.
The South Staffordshire.

The North Staffordshire.
The Duke of Beaufort's.
The Cotswold.
The Dumfriesshire.
The Albrighton.
The North Cotswold.

#### PART VI.

Lord Middleton's.
The Sinnington.
The Wheatland.
The United Pack.
The Chiddingfold.

Lord Fitzhardinge's.
Hon. Mark Rolle's.
South-and-West Wilts.
Lord Portman's.
The Cleveland.

The North Durham.
Braes of Derwent.
The Radnorshire and West Hereford.
The Monmouthshire.

*Each part is published separately, price 2s. 6d.*

"THE FIELD" OFFICE, 346, STRAND, W.C.

A CATALOGUE OF BOOKS

*Price 1s., by post 1s. 1d.*

## TATTERSALL'S RULES ON BETTING,

### WITH EXPLANATORY NOTES AND COMMENTS,

Containing an Account of Cases decided by Tattersall's Committee, with a Copious Index, and the Rules of Racing appended.

By G. HERBERT STUTFIELD, Barrister-at-Law.

Author of the "Law Relating to Betting, Time Bargains, and Gaming."

---

*Post 8vo., price 7s. 6d., by post 8s.*

## Moss from a Rolling Stone:

### OR,

### MOORISH WANDERINGS AND RAMBLING REMINISCENCES.

BY

### CHARLES A. PAYTON,

"Sarcelle" of "The Field," Author of "The Diamond Diggings of South Africa." &c.

---

*Price 5s. cloth, by post 5s. 4d.*

## A Year of Liberty; or, Salmon Angling in Ireland.

BY

### W. PEARD M.D., LL.B

---

*Price 8d., by post 9d.*

## THE "FIELD"
## LAWN TENNIS UMPIRES' SCORE-SHEET BOOK

(Sixty Sets),

WITH INSTRUCTIONS FOR THE USE OF UMPIRES.

Adapted for the Use of Umpires, as used at the Championship Meetings.

---

"THE FIELD" OFFICE, 346, STRAND, W.C.

PUBLISHED BY HORACE COX. 19

*Price 3s. 6d., by post 3s. 10d.*

# The Archer's Register
## For 1889-90.
### Edited by F. T. FOLLETT,
*Archery Correspondent of "The Field."*

---

*Royal 8vo, price 10s. 6d., by post 11s.*

## HORSE BREEDING RECOLLECTIONS.
### BY
### COUNT G. LEHNDORFF,

Containing Notes on the Breeding of Thoroughbreds—In-breeding and Out-crossing—Pedigrees of all the Principal Sires—and Genealogical Tables of Celebrated Thoroughbreds.

---

*Crown 8vo., profusely Illustrated, price 2s. 6d.*

## GIPSY TENTS, AND HOW TO USE THEM.
### BY G. R. LOWNDES.

---

*In post 8vo., with Illustrations, price 3s. 6d., by post 3s. 9d.*

## The Practical Management of Fisheries.
### A BOOK FOR PROPRIETORS AND KEEPERS.
### By the late FRANCIS FRANCIS,
*Author of "Fish Culture," "A Book on Angling," "Reports on Salmon Ladders," &c.*

### CONTENTS.

Chap.
- I.—Fish and Fish Food.
- II.—How to Grow Fish Food and how to Make Fishes' Homes.
- III.—On the Management of Weeds and the Economy of Fishing.
- IV.—The Enemies of Trout and how to Circumvent them.
- V.—The Artificial Incubation of Ova.

Chap.
- VI.—On the Rearing of Fry and the Conduct of Ponds, Stews, &c.
- VII.—Some Hatcheries.
- VIII.—Coarse Fish.
- IX.—On Salmon and Trout Ladders and Passes.
- APPENDIX.—Notes, &c.

---

"THE FIELD" OFFICE, 346, STRAND, W.C.

*Crown 8vo., price 2s. 6d., by post 2s. 9d.*

## PUBLIC SHOOTING QUARTERS
### IN ENGLAND, WALES, SCOTLAND, IRELAND, AND ON THE CONTINENT.

### BY "WILDFOWLER."
Author of "Shooting and Fishing Trips," "Modern Wildfowling," "Table of Loads," &c.

*Price 1s., by post 1s. 1d.*

## NOTES ON THE PROOF OF GUNS.
TOGETHER WITH THE NEW RULES AND SCALES OF PROOF PASSED BY THE SECRETARY FOR WAR, AND COMMENTS THEREON.

---

REPORTS on SALMON LADDERS, with Original Drawings, Plans, and Sections. By the late FRANCIS FRANCIS. In post 4to., price 2s. 6d., by post 2s. 7d.

---

A MANUAL of the LAW of SALMON FISHERIES in ENGLAND and WALES, with a copious Index. By SPENCER WALPOLE, one of Her Majesty's Inspectors of Salmon Fisheries. Price 2s. 6d., by post 2s. 8d.

---

A TABLE of CALCULATIONS for use with the "Field" Force Gauge for Testing Shot Guns. Also an Illustration and Description of the Apparatus. In demy 4to., price 2s. 6d.

---

SIXTY-FIFTH HALF-YEARLY ISSUE.

THE COURSING CALENDAR, for the Spring Season 1890, contains Returns of all the Public Courses run in Great Britain and Ireland. A revised List of Addresses of Coursing Secretaries, Public Coursers, Judges, Slippers, and Trainers, with List of Waterloo Cup Winners, Greyhound Sales, &c. Edited by C. M. BROWNE ("ROBIN HOOD"). Price 10s. 6d.

---

THE RULES of PIGEON SHOOTING. Published by Special Permission, the Hurlingham Club and the Gun Club Rules of Pigeon Shooting. SECOND EDITION. Bound together in cloth, gilt edges, price 6d., by post 7d.

---

**Official Edition of the Laws of Lawn Tennis.**
*Now ready, price 6d., by post 7d.*

THE LAWS of LAWN TENNIS for the Year 1890, issued under the authority of the Lawn Tennis Association.

---

**Official Edition of the Regulations for the Management of Lawn Tennis Prize Meetings.**
*Now ready, price 6d., by post 7d.*

REGULATIONS for the MANAGEMENT of LAWN TENNIS PRIZE MEETINGS and INTER-COUNTY and INTER-CLUB MEETINGS, issued under the authority of the Lawn Tennis Association.

---

"THE FIELD" OFFICE, 346, STRAND, W.C.

PUBLISHED BY HORACE COX. 21

*Price 2s. 6d., by post 2s. 9d.*

# GAME REGISTER,

GIVING AN ACCOUNT OF EACH HEAD OF GAME KILLED, AND HOW DISPOSED OF.

Containing also Divisions for Registering Sporting Engagements and General Observations.

THIRD EDITION, ENLARGED AND REVISED. *Large post 8vo., with Illustrations, price 5s. cloth, by post 5s. 4d.*

## THE COUNTRY HOUSE:

A COLLECTION OF USEFUL INFORMATION AND RECIPES,

Adapted to the Country Gentleman and his household, and of the greatest utility to the housekeeper generally.

BY I. E. B. C.,

Editor of "Facts and Useful Hints relating to Fishing and Shooting," and "The Gamekeeper's and Game Preserver's Account Book and Diary."

PUBLISHED ANNUALLY. *In post 8vo., price 1s. 6d., by post 1s. 8d.*

## THE ANGLER'S DIARY

AND

## TOURIST FISHERMAN'S GAZETTEER

CONTAINS

A Record of the Rivers and Lakes of the World, to which is added a List of Rivers of Great Britain, with their nearest Railway Stations.
Also Forms for Registering the Fish taken during the year; as well as the Time of the Close Seasons and Angling Licences.

BY I. E. B. C.,

Editor of "The Gamekeeper's and Game Preserver's Account Book and Diary," &c.

THIRD EDITION. *In fcap. 8vo., price 1s., by post 1s. 1d.*

## WILD BIRDS' PROTECTION ACT, 1880,

WITH COMMENTS ON THE RESPECTIVE SECTIONS

Explanatory of their bearing as regards owners and occupiers of land, sportsmen, bird catchers, bird dealers, &c.; together with Notes on the Birds named in the Schedule, their provincial names, &c.

"An accurate exposition of and commentary on the recent measure, and will dispel many misconceptions of its scope."—*Quarterly Review.*
"A capital annotated edition of the Act."—*Saturday Review.*

"You have not the book of riddles about you have you?"—*Merry Wives.*

*Price 5s., by post 5s. 3d.*

## "Whetstones for Wits;" or, Double Acrostics.

BY

## VARIOUS HANDS.

Edited by "CRACK."

"THE FIELD" OFFICE, 346, STRAND, W.C.

*Demy 8vo., price 5s. 6d., by post 5s. 10d.*

THE

# ROTHAMSTED EXPERIMENTS

ON THE

## GROWTH OF WHEAT, BARLEY,

AND THE

## MIXED HERBAGE OF GRASS LAND.

BY WILLIAM FREAM, B.Sc. LOND., F.L.S., F.G.S., F.S.S.

---

THIRD EDITION. *In demy 8vo., price 10s. 6d., by post 11s.*

# ESTATE MANAGEMENT:

A Practical Handbook for Landlords, Agents, and Pupils.

BY CHARLES E. CURTIS.

WITH A

LEGAL SUPPLEMENT BY A BARRISTER.

---

*Extract from Preface.*—"He who intends to qualify himself for such interesting and responsible work as the care and oversight of landed property must, in these days of keen competition, give up the idea that he need only abandon himself to the pleasures of a country life, and that all needful information will be picked up by the way."

## CONTENTS.

Chap.
- I.—Letting and Leases.
- II.—Farm Valuations.
- III.—Forestry.
- IV.—Underwood.
- V.—Fences.
- VI.—Grasses suitable for Woods and Plantations.
- VII.—The Home Farm.

Chap.
- VIII.} Repairs and Materials.
- IX.  }
- X.—The Blights of Wheat and other Cereals.
- XI.—Accounts.
- XII.—Useful Rules of Arithmetic and Mensuration.

---

*In crown 8vo., price 1s., by post 1s. 1d.*

# CATECHISM OF ESTATE MANAGEMENT.

SECTION I.

## LETTING AND LEASES.

BY CHAS. E. CURTIS, F.S.I.,

Professor of Estate Management at the College of Agriculture, Principal of the School of Estate Management, Author of "Estate Management," &c.

---

"THE FIELD" OFFICE, 346, STRAND, W.C.

PUBLISHED BY HORACE COX.

*Price 6s., by post 6s. 6d.*

SECOND EDITION, Greatly Enlarged (with Illustrations and Plans of Silos).

# SILOS

## FOR

## PRESERVING BRITISH FODDER CROPS STORED IN A GREEN STATE.

### NOTES ON THE ENSILAGE OF GRASSES, CLOVERS, VETCHES, &c.

*Compiled and Annotated*
BY THE
**EDITOR OF "THE FIELD."**

### CONTENTS.

INTRODUCTORY.—Cattle-feeding v. corn-growing; previous information on the storage of green fodder in pits; silos in ancient and modern times.

CHAP.
I.—Summary of Practice.
II.—CROPS FOR THE SILO.—Grasses, clovers, lucerne, vetches, maize, green rye and oats, spurrey, buckwheat, comfrey, roots, and miscellaneous crops.
III.—THE VARIOUS KINDS OF SILOS.—Earthen pits and other simple forms of silos; barn and other converted silos; specially constructed silos of stone, brick, concrete, wood, &c.; ensilage stacks and barrels.
IV.—COST OF SILOS.—Estimation of capacity cost of British silos, specially constructed; converted buildings; patent silos of concrete slabs, slate, and wood; French silos; relative capacity and cost of silos and hay-barns; roofs.
V.—FILLING THE SILO.—Mixture of dry material with green fodder; influence of wet weather; chopping up the fodder; slow v. quick filling; curbs or super-silos; the use of salt; trampling down the fodder.
VI.—COVERING AND CLOSING THE SILO.—Straw and other materials; the covering boards; closing the doorway.
VII.—WEIGHTING THE SILO.—Amount of weight to put on; consequences of insufficient pressure; expression of juice from the fodder; mechanical arrangements for pressure; cost of apparatus.
VIII.—OPENING THE SILO.—Precautions to be taken in uncovering the silage, and removing the weights.
IX.—EFFECT OF ENSILAGE ON FODDERS.—Fermentation in the pit; advantages and losses produced by fermentation; reduction in weight and altered proportion of constituents of silage, resulting from excessive fermentation.
X.—FEEDING QUALITIES OF SILAGE.—Effect of amount of moisture in diluting the nutrient matters; comparative money value of green fodders and silage; results of feeding experiments on the condition of the animals and the production of milk and cream; silage for horses, sheep, &c.
XI.—EFFECT OF SILAGE ON DAIRY PRODUCE.—Complaints of bad flavour in milk and butter; causes of conflicting reports.
XII.—COST OF HAYMAKING V. ENSILAGE.—Differences of cost of the process under various conditions.

*Price 6d., by post 7d.*

## SHORT NOTES ON SILO EXPERIMENTS AND PRACTICE.

(Extracted from "Silos or Preserving British Fodder Crops.")

*Price 6d., by post 7d.; or 2s. 6d. the half-dozen., by post 2s. 11d.*

## "THE FIELD" DUPLICATE JUDGING BOOK

Facilitates the work of the Judges at Poultry and other Shows, by a very simple method of entering and preserving a duplicate judging list.

"THE FIELD" OFFICE, 346, STRAND, W.C.

Price 6d., by post 7d.

# HARVESTING CROPS INDEPENDENTLY OF WEATHER.

Practical Notes on the "Neilson System" of Harvesting.

### By "AGRICOLA"
### AND OTHER CONTRIBUTORS OF "THE FIELD" NEWSPAPER.

---

*In crown 8vo., price 2s. 6d., by post 2s. 8d.*

# MANURES:

### Their Respective Merits from an Economical Point of View.

### By A. W. CREWS,

Author of "Guano: its Origin, History, and Virtues," "The Potato and its Cultivation," &c.

---

### CONTENTS.

PART I.—Definition of the Word "Manure"—Nature's Modes of Applying Fertilisers—History—Classification.

PART II.—The Value of Ploughing Down Green Crops—Weeds—Sea-weed—Straw—Sawdust—Tanners' Bark—Wood Ashes—Peat—Rape Cake—Hemp—Poppy, Cotton, and Cocoa-nut Cakes—Bran—Malt Dust—Brewers' Grains—Coal—Soot—Charcoal.

PART III.—Dead Animals—Fish—Blood—Animalised Charcoal—Bones—Horn—Woollen Rags, Hairs, Feathers, &c.—Night-soil—Farm-yard Manure—Guano.

PART IV.—Salts of Ammonia—Salts of Magnesia—Salts of Potash—Salts of Soda—Common Salt—Lime and its Compounds—"Ooze."

---

*In crown 8vo., price 2s., by post 2s. 2d.*

# THE POTATO AND ITS CULTIVATION.

### By A. W. CREWS,

Author of "Guano: its Origin, History, and Virtues," "Manures: their Respective Merits," &c.

---

### CONTENTS.

Derivation — History — Constituents — Varieties — Sprouting — Soils — Planting— Manures— Earthing up— Disease — Scab — Storing— Forcing — Producing New Varieties—Substitutes for the "Potato"—Miscellaneous Information.

---

Price 1s., by post 1s. 1d.

# HOW TO GROW AND CURE ENGLISH TOBACCO.

### By H. KAINS-JACKSON.

---

"THE FIELD" OFFICE, 346, STRAND, W.C.

*Demy 8vo., price 3s. 6d., by post 3s. 9d., Illustrated with several Diagrams.*

## THE
# PRACTICAL SURVEYOR:
### A TREATISE UPON SURVEYING.

SPECIALLY ARRANGED FOR THE GUIDANCE OF PUPILS, STEWARDS, THE SCHOLASTIC PROFESSION, AND INTENDING EMIGRANTS.

### By THOMAS HOLLOWAY.

**CONTENTS.**

CHAP.
- I.—The Man and his Outfit.
- II.—The Chain — Cautions to Beginners — Best Figure for Chain Surveying.
- III.—Boundaries.
- IV.—Setting-out Lines by the Eye and passing Obstructions.
- V.—Division of the Circle and Use of Box Sextant—Chain Angles Condemned—Cross Staff Condemned—The Optical Square—Measuring Inaccessible Distances.
- VI.—The Theodolite—Setting-out Lines with the Theodolite.
- VII.—Reduction of the Measure of Undulating Ground to Horizontal Measures and Table of Vertical Angles.
- VIII.—Measuring Lines — The Offset Staff and taking Offsets.
- IX.—To Prove the Correctness of Observations taken with the Sextant — Single Fields Measured with the Chain and Optical Square, so that the Areas can be directly Calculated.
- X.—To Set-out a Right Angle with the Chain—Figures of the Lines of Measurement best adapted to Irregular Fields.
- XI.—Equalising Boundaries, and Drawing a Triangle equal to a given Figure.
- XII.—Computation of Arrears of Irregular Fields.

CHAP.
- XIII.—Example of a Survey of several Fields together, and the Field Book.
- XIV.—Reference Numbers to Maps — To put Detached Buildings in correct Positions on a Plan by Means of Unmeasured Lines—Lines Measured on the Work—Making Stations.
- XV.—Plotting — Selection and Management of Paper—Inking In.
- XVI.—Surveys made for the purpose of Dividing Land into Stated Quantities.
- XVII.—Setting-out Allotments and Building Plots.
- XVIII.—Angles and Bearings, and Use and Adjustment of Circular Protractor.
- XIX.—Traverse Surveys.
- XX.—Trespass.
- XXI.—Quality Lines—Superstructures and Works Underground — Harvest and Coppice Work—Reducing Plans from a Large Plan to a Small One.
- XXII.—To Copy a Map—Colouring, Penmanship, &c.
- XXIII.—Commencement of a Parish Survey—Surveying to a Scale of Feet.
- XXIV.—Town Surveying.
- XXV.—Testing the Accuracy of a Survey—General Remarks.
- XXVI.—In Memory of the Past.

*Price 1s., by post, 1s. 1d.*

## PASTURES, OLD AND NEW:
A Plea for the Improvement of Old Turf, Better Systems of Grassing-down, and the Prolonged Tenure of Alternate Husbandry Grass Layers.

### By JOSEPH DARBY.

*In crown 8vo., with Thirteen full-page Plates, price 2s. 6d., by post 2s. 9d.*

## The Swimming Instructor:
### A TREATISE ON THE ARTS OF SWIMMING AND DIVING.

### By WILLIAM WILSON,
Author of "Swimming, Diving, and How to Save Life," "The Bather's Manual," "Hints on Swimming."

"THE FIELD" OFFICE, 346, STRAND, W.C.

SECOND EDITION. *In Three Parts, large post 8vo., price 5s., by post* **5s. 4d.** each Part.

THE

# FARM, GARDEN, AND STABLE.

By I. E. B. C.,

Editor of "The Gamekeeper's and Game Preserver's Account Book and Diary."

## CONTENTS.

**Part I.—The Farm. 5s. 4d. by Post.**
Cattle—Crops—Dairy—Diseases—Fencing—Food for Stock—Manures—Miscellaneous—Pigs—Sheep—Soils—Weeds—Woods.

**Part II.—The Garden. 5s. 4d. by Post.**
Flowers—Fruit—Houses—Lawns—Manures—Miscellaneous—Seeds—Trees and Shrubs—Vegetables—Vermin—Weeds.

**Part III.—The Stable. 5s. 4d. by Post.**
Carriages—Diseases—Feeding—Harness, &c.—Miscellaneous—Stable Management.

---

PUBLISHED ANNUALLY. *In large post 8vo.*

THE

# KENNEL CLUB STUD BOOK:

CONTAINING A COMPLETE

## RECORD OF DOG SHOWS AND FIELD TRIALS,

WITH

### PEDIGREES OF SPORTING AND NON-SPORTING DOGS.

Vol. I., from 1859 to 1873, price 12s. 6d., by post 13s.

Price 10s. 6d., by post 10s. 10d. each—

Vol. III., 1875; Vol. IV., 1876; Vol. V., 1877; Vol. VI., 1878; Vol. VII., 1879; Vol. VIII., 1880; Vol. IX., 1881; Vol. XI., 1883; Vol. XII., 1884; Vol. XIII., 1885; Vol. XIV., 1886; Vol. XV., 1887; Vol. XVI., 1888; Vol. XVII., 1889.

---

SECOND EDITION. *Price 2s. 6d., free by post 2s. 8d.*

# PRACTICAL DINNERS:

## CONTAINING 108 MENUS, AND 584 RECIPES.

By "The G. C.,"

AUTHOR OF "ROUND THE TABLE."

"It is difficult even for a literary critic to read a cookery book straight through, but we have tested a few of the recipes, and those have been very good."—*Athenæum.*

"To those who wish to raise gastronomy into a fine art, the suggestions of the author will be acceptable, for if the everyday fare of ordinary mortals is to be prepared by 'The G. C.'s' recipes, the result will be a repast suitable to the palate of Lucullus. A variety of new savouries are also given."—*Morning Post.*

"Quite up to the level of a good cook's respectful attention, or an epicure's critical regard. . . . Reducing fine cookery to the understanding of ordinary intelligence. From all reproach of ignorant pretension this manual of plain directions is free. . . . The reader will find in these pages a choice of dishes, not one of which is inadequately or erroneously formulated."—*Daily Telegraph,* April 28, 1887.

---

"THE FIELD" OFFICE, 346, STRAND, W.C.

PUBLISHED BY HORACE COX.

*Published Annually, about December, price 1s., by post 1s. 2d.*

# THE RURAL ALMANAC

AND

## SPORTSMAN'S ILLUSTRATED CALENDAR FOR 1890.

*Articles on the following Subjects are included in the List of Contents:*

THE PAST RACING SEASON.
LIST OF HUNTS, THEIR MASTERS, &c.
CANINE MATTERS IN 1889.
DOG TRIALS IN 1889.
LISTS OF OTTERHOUNDS AND DOG CLUBS.
GUNS OF OUR ANCESTORS.
BREECHLOADERS OF THE PAST.
SIZES OF SHOT AND THEIR VELOCITIES.
TRAPS FOR CATCHING PHEASANTS.
THAMES TROUT SEASON.
TRAINING THE GOSHAWK.
THE LEADING CRICKET COUNTIES IN 1889.
THE CULTURE OF ASPARAGUS.
PRESERVING EGGS FOR TWELVE MONTHS.
SHEEP ON DAIRY FARMS.
FARM FRUITS.
THE PAST TENNIS SEASON.
YACHT RACING IN 1889.
STALLIONS FOR BREEDING BLOODSTOCK AND HUNTERS
  (List of about 300 Stallions, with their Pedigrees, and Fees for Thoroughbred and Half-Bred Mares).

ALSO SUMMARIES, TABLES, RECIPES, &c., VIZ.,

Angling close seasons
Artificial fox earth
Athletic Championships
Beagles, packs of
Bicycling, best times on record
Birch wine
Boat-races, Oxford and Cambridge
Cambridgeshire winners
Cesarewitch winners
Close seasons for game
Derby winners
Distinct vision under water
Dog clubs, list of

Earwigs
Flowers as an article of food
Foxhounds, packs of
Game, legal season for killing
Gorse coverts
Harriers, packs of
Huntsmen, changes of
Jumping records
Lawn tennis courts
Oaks winners
Otter hounds, packs of
Public Schools athletics in 1889
Races of 1889, dates of

Racquets, Schools challenge cup
Running, best times
St. Leger winners
Swimming, amateur performances
Tennis, University matches
Trapping rats with gins
Ticks in dogs
Tricycling performances
University athletic sports
University boat-races
University racquet matches
University tennis matches
Walking, best times.

"THE FIELD" OFFICE, 346, STRAND, W.C.

# A CATALOGUE OF BOOKS

*In crown 8vo., price 3s. 6d., by post 3s. 9d.*

## ANGLING REMINISCENCES.

### By the late FRANCIS FRANCIS.

CONTENTS.

A Christmas Retrospect; Luck; Loch Tay; The Angler's Wish; Spring Salmon Fishing; Grayling Fishing; Barbel Fishing; Cover Shooting; Fly Fishing for Ladies; Saint Mayfly; My First Salmon; The Mayfly Mess; A Month in the West; Trout Fishing; In and Out Dales; Up and Down; Tom Bowers's Christmas.

---

FOURTH EDITION. *In demy 4to., on toned paper, and in fancy cover, price 2s., by post 2s. 2d.*

## THE BOOK OF DINNER SERVIETTES

CONTAINS

### A New Introduction on the Decoration of Dinner Tables, and General Directions for Folding the Serviettes.

There are Twenty-one different kinds given, with Ninety-two Woodcuts illustrative of the various Folds required, and the Serviettes complete.

---

*Price 5s., by post 5s. 2d.*

## "COMBINED FIGURE SKATING;"

BEING

### A COLLECTION OF 300 COMBINED FIGURES, AS SKATED BY THE SKATING CLUB, LONDON, THE WIMBLEDON SKATING CLUB, &c.

Illustrated by 130 scaled diagrams, showing the correct direction of every curve executed by the skater, and the recognised amount of circling round the centre: together with a progressive series of alternate "calls."

The figures are named in accordance with the revised system of nomenclature and rules of combined figure skating, compiled by the Skating Club, London, Sept. 11, 1882.

Diagrams of the combined figures in the first and second class tests of the National Skating Association are included.

### BY MONTAGU S. F. MONIER-WILLIAMS AND STANLEY F. MONIER-WILLIAMS
(Members of the Wimbledon Skating Club).

---

"THE FIELD" OFFICE, 346, STRAND, W.C.

PUBLISHED BY HORACE COX.

*In crown 8vo., price 5s., by post 5s. 4d.*

# BOAT-RACING;
## OR,
## The ARTS of ROWING and TRAINING.
### BY
### EDWIN DAMPIER BRICKWOOD.
(EX-AMATEUR CHAMPION OF THE THAMES.)

### CONTENTS.

**ROWING.**

CHAP.
- I.—Introduction: Past and Present Condition of Boatracing.
- II.—Racing Boats: Their History and Fittings.
- III.—The Sliding Seat: Its Invention, Adoption, and Theory.
- IV.—How to Use an Oar, and Sculls.
- V.—Faults and Errors: What to avoid.
- VI.—Steering: Coxswain and Non-coxswain.
- VII.—Teaching Beginners.
- VIII.—Coaching for Races, and Selection of Crews.
- IX.—The Varieties and Conduct of Boatraces.
- X.—The Laws of Boatracing.

CHAP.
- XI.—The Qualifications of Amateurs.
- XII.—Boat Clubs: Their Organisation and Administration.
- XIII.—Historical Records, A.D. 1715 to 1838.
- XIV.— ,,    ,,    A.D. 1839 to 1855.
- XV.— ,,    ,,    A.D. 1856 to 1875.

**TRAINING.**
- XVI.—Its Principles.
- XVII.—Its Practice.
- XVIII.—Prohibitions, Ailments, &c.
- APPENDIX.—Rules for Betting.
- INDEX.

*Published Annually, price 1s., by post 1s. 1d.*

# THE ROWING ALMANACK AND OARSMAN'S COMPANION.
## Edited by E. D. BRICKWOOD
(EX-AMATEUR CHAMPION OF THE THAMES),
*Author of "Boat-Racing; or, the Arts of Rowing and Training."*

### CONTENTS.

- A Calendar with Space for Memoranda and High Water Table, with a Table of Tidal Observations.
- Rules and Regulations of Punting.
- Record of all Regattas and principal Club Races, with a copious Index.
- A Review of the Rowing Season.
- An Itinerary of the River Thames from Oxford to Putney, showing all the points of interest, with Hotels, &c.
- A Rowing Directory.
- The Lengths of the different Racing Courses.
- The Laws of Boat Racing.
- Boat Racing Legislation.
- The Championship of the World.
- The Rule of the Road on the River.
- Thames Navigation Rules.
- Tables of Winners of all the principal Races and Regattas.

*Post free, 6d., cloth gilt.*

# RULES OF THE GAME OF HOCKEY
### AND OF
## THE HOCKEY ASSOCIATION.

SECOND EDITION. *Price 2s. 6d., by post 2s. 8d., in limp cloth.*

# RABBITS FOR PROFIT AND RABBITS FOR POWDER.

A Treatise upon the New Industry of Hutch Rabbit Farming in the Open, and upon Warrens specially intended for Sporting purposes; with Hints as to their Construction, Cost, and Maintenance.

### BY R. J. LLOYD PRICE.

"THE FIELD" OFFICE, 346, STRAND, W.C.

A CATALOGUE OF BOOKS

*Price One Shilling; by Post, 1s. 3d.*

# THE QUEEN ALMANAC,
AND
## LADY'S CALENDAR, 1890.

AMONG ITS CONTENTS WILL BE FOUND

## A CHROMO-LITHOGRAPH PLATE OF DESIGNS
### FOR EMBROIDERY ON SATIN, &c.
A SUPPLEMENT OF DESIGNS FOR BENT IRON OR BRASS WORK, with Instructions.
A COLOURED SUPPLEMENT OF NOVELTIES IN CROCHET WORK,

*Artistic Furniture and Fittings; the Feast of Roses at the Botanical Gardens, July 15, 1889; Decorative Floral Arrangements; Decorative China and Pottery; Specimens of Silhouette Work; Specimens of Pen and Ink Work; How to Restore Faience and Porcelain; Prize Fans; Tableaux Vivants, &c.*

### THIRTY-SIX PORTRAITS:
Among others, Portraits of the Duchess of Fife, Duke and Duchess of Sparta, the Grand Duke and Grand Duchess Paul of Russia, the Archduke Franz Salvator and Archduchess Marie Valerie of Austria, the Marchioness of Lansdowne, &c.

ALSO

Dinner and Ball Toilettes; Ornaments for the Hair; Tea Jackets, Tea Gowns, and Evening Dresses; Ladies' Winter Coats, Capes, and Hats; Ladies' Promenade Costumes; Girls' Morning Costumes and Dancing Frocks; Girls' Outdoor Costumes and Winter Hats; Aprons, Lingerie, and Underlinen; Child's Frock, Aprons, and Fichus, &c.

Full information is given relating to—The Royal Family; the Royal Household; the Government; British and Foreign Ambassadors; Lords Lieutenants of Counties in the United Kingdom; Irish and Scotch Representative Peers; Peers who are Minors; Peeresses in their own right; Alphabetical List of the Surnames of the Peers Temporal; Complete List of the House of Peers, with their Surnames and Titles, and the Titles of their Eldest Sons; Jewish Calendar; Bank of England; Post Office Regulations; Eclipses in 1890; List of Charities, Associations, &c.; Obituary of Ladies of Distinction during the Past Year.

RECIPES FOR HORS D'ŒUVRES, TASTY WAYS OF COOKING FISH, CURRIES, &c.

EIGHTH YEAR OF PUBLICATION.
*Now ready, fcap. 8vo., price 1s. 6d., by post 1s. 9d., pp. 400.*

## THE LAWN-TENNIS CALENDAR
### FOR 1890.
EDITED BY B. C. EVELEGH (OF "THE FIELD.").

THE ITALIAN SYSTEM of BEE KEEPING; being an Exposition of Don Giotto Ulivi's Economical Frame Hives and Honey Extractor. By ARTHUR J. DANYELL, late Capt. H.M. 31st Regiment. With Illustrations. Price 1s., by post 1s. 1d. This pamphlet contains practical directions for the making and utilisation of frame hives, costing less than 2s. each, and a centrifugal honey extractor costing 5s. or 6s.

"THE QUEEN" OFFICE, 346, STRAND, W.C.

PUBLISHED BY HORACE COX. 31

*In 4to., printed on toned paper, with plates, price 5s., by post 5s. 4d.*

# THE QUEEN LACE BOOK:
## AN
## HISTORICAL AND DESCRIPTIVE ACCOUNT OF THE HAND-MADE ANTIQUE LACES OF ALL COUNTRIES.

### By L. W.

This work contains the whole of the series of articles on Antique Point Lace which have been published in "The Queen." It will prove an invaluable guide and book of reference to ladies interested in Antique Lace, and, with its highly ornamental embossed cover, will form a handsome ornament for the drawing-room table.

---

ENGLISH TRANSLATIONS OF THE CLASSICS.

*Post 8vo., 540 pages, price 7s. 6d.*

## HALF-HOURS WITH GREEK AND LATIN AUTHORS,
### FROM VARIOUS ENGLISH TRANSLATIONS, WITH BIOGRAPHICAL NOTICES.

### By G. H. JENNINGS and W. S. JOHNSTONE,
Authors of "A Book of Parliamentary Anecdote."

---

*In post 8vo., price 5s., by post 5s. 4d.*

# THE BARB AND THE BRIDLE:
## A
## HANDBOOK of EQUITATION for LADIES,
### AND
MANUAL OF INSTRUCTION IN THE SCIENCE OF RIDING FROM THE PREPARATORY SUPPLING EXERCISES ON FOOT TO THE FORM IN WHICH A LADY SHOULD RIDE TO HOUNDS.

### By "VIEILLE MOUSTACHE."

---

*Handsomely bound in cloth, price 3s. 6d., by post 3s. 9d.*

## ACTING CHARADES FOR OLD AND YOUNG.
### BY ARTHUR LILLIE,
Author of "The Enchanted Toasting Fork," &c.

---

*In paper cover, price 6d.*

# "THE QUEEN" RECIPES.
By "THE G. C.," Author of "Round the Table."

---

"THE QUEEN" OFFICE, 346, STRAND, W.C.

# INDEX TO BOOKS.

| | PAGE | | PAGE |
|---|---|---|---|
| Angling | 13 | Lawn Tennis Score Book | 18 |
| Angler's Diary | 21 | Lawn Tennis Regulations | 20 |
| Angling Reminiscences | 28 | Lawn Tennis Calendar | 30 |
| Annals of Tennis | 13 | Manures | 24 |
| Archer's Register | 19 | Management of Fisheries | 19 |
| Art of Skating | 6 | Modern Sportman's Gun, &c., Vol. I. | 10 |
| Betting Rules | 18 | Ditto Ditto Vol. II. | 11 |
| British and Irish Fishes | 3 | Modern Wildfowling | 14 |
| Boat Racing | 29 | Moss from a Rolling Stone | 18 |
| Barb and Bridle | 31 | Pastures Old and New | 25 |
| Charades | 31 | Pheasant Book | 3 |
| Cattle of Great Britain | 6 | Pheasant Rearing | 15 |
| Cattle, Sheep, and Pigs | 7 | Pigeon Shooting Rules | 20 |
| Coursing Calendar | 20 | Potatoes | 24 |
| Catechism of Estates | 22 | Practical Dinners | 26 |
| Colorado | 16 | Practical Surveyor | 25 |
| Collie or Sheep Dog | 10 | Proof of Guns, Notes on | 20 |
| Combined Figure Skating | 28 | Public Shooting Quarters | 20 |
| Country House | 21 | Queen Almanac | 30 |
| Dinner Serviette Book | 28 | Queen Lace Book | 31 |
| Dogs of the British Islands | 8 | Queen Recipes, Part I. | 31 |
| Early Maturity of Live Stock | 16 | Rabbits | 29 |
| English Game of Cricket | 12 | Rambles after Sport | 16 |
| English Tobacco | 24 | Rothamsted Experiments | 22 |
| Estate Management | 22 | Rowing Almanac | 29 |
| Essays on Sport | 16 | Rural Almanac | 27 |
| Farm | 26 | Salmon Laws | 20 |
| Figure Skating | 6 | Salmon Ladders | 20 |
| Fox Terrier | 10 | Salmonidæ | 3 |
| Game Register | 21 | Sheep and Pigs | 6 |
| Garden | 26 | Shifts and Expedients of Camp Life | 9 |
| Gipsy Tents, and How to Use Them | 19 | Silos | 23 |
| Golfing Annual | 9 | Silo Experiments | 23 |
| Half Hours | 31 | Sketches, &c., in Norway | 15 |
| Harvesting Crops | 24 | Sporting Sketches | 11 |
| Hints on Hawks | 16 | Stable | 26 |
| Hockey Rules | 29 | Swimming Instructor | 25 |
| Horse Breeding | 19 | Table of Calculations | 20 |
| Hot Pot | 13 | Twenty-six Years, &c. | 14 |
| Hunting Countries | 17 | Wild Birds Protection Act | 21 |
| Idstone Papers | 8 | Whetstones for Wits | 21 |
| Italian System of Beekeeping | 30 | Yacht and Boat Sailing | 5 |
| Judging Books | 23 | Yacht Racing Calendar | 4 |
| Kennel Club Stud Book | 26 | Year of Liberty | 18 |
| Lawn Tennis Laws | 20 | | |

PUBLISHED AT 346, STRAND, W.C.

*Advertisements.*

# THE FIELD,

## THE COUNTRY GENTLEMAN'S NEWSPAPER.

*Published every Saturday, price Sixpence.*

**LEADERS**
ON interesting Sporting subjects are given every week in THE FIELD.

**"SHOOTING."**
CONTENTS: Original Articles and Correspondence on Shooting Adventures, Game Preservation, New Guns, Cartridges, and all the paraphernalia of a sportsman.

**"ANGLING."**
ARTICLES and Correspondence on Fishing, Reports from the Rivers, Fish Preservation and Culture, and all matters connected with river, lake, or sea fishing.

**"HUNTING."**
DESCRIPTION of Hunting Countries, reports of Runs with the various Packs of Hounds, Hunting Appointments, Visits to the Kennels, Notes from the Shires, &c., are given during the season.

**"THE TURF."**
REPORTS of all the principal Race and Steeplechase Meetings are given, together with Notes and Anticipations on Future Events, Sales of Blood Stock, &c.

**"COURSING."**
REPORTS of all Meetings are given weekly for the duration of the season.

**"DOGS AND HORSES."**
ARTICLES and Correspondence on the above subjects, Reports of Horse and Dog Shows, &c.

**"THE VETERINARIAN"**
GIVES full and practical instruction for the management of Cattle in health and disease.

**"THE COUNTRY HOUSE."**
UNDER this heading will be found Articles, Notes, Queries, &c., on all Subjects and Inventions that concern the Country House.

**"POULTRY AND PIGEONS."**
ARTICLES on their management, accounts of Pigeon Races, &c.

**"ARCHERY."**
ALL the principal Matches throughout the United Kingdom are reported during the season.

**A CHESS PROBLEM**
IS given constantly, with annotated Games, and Chess news.

**"GOLF."**
REPORTS of Golf Contests, Description of Links, &c.

**"LAWN TENNIS."**
REPORTS of all the principal Matches, and Notes on the Formation of Courts, &c.

**"SWIMMING."**
FULL REPORTS of all the principal Contests of the Season.

**"YACHTING."**
ARTICLES on Yacht Building, Reports of Matches, Accounts of Cruises, Correspondence, Yacht Intelligence, &c.

**"ROWING."**
REPORTS of Matches and Regattas, Articles on Training.

**"ATHLETIC SPORTS"**
ARE fully reported every week during the season.

**"FOOTBALL"**
REPORTS of Association and Rugby Matches during the season.

**"BICYCLING AND TRICYCLING."**
REPORTS of the principal Races, Descriptions of New Machines, Accounts of Tours, &c.

**"CRICKET."**
FULL and accurate Reports of all Matches of interest are given during the season.

**"TRAVEL AND COLONISATION"**
CONTAINS Articles upon Explorations in little known parts of the world, their capabilities for colonisation, stock-raising, sport, &c.

**"THE FARM"**
GIVES practical advice for the proper management of Farms (both arable and pasture) and Farm Stock, Reports of Agricultural Shows, Sales of Shorthorns, &c.

**"THE GARDEN."**
PRACTICAL instruction for laying out and managing Flower and Kitchen Gardens, Grape Houses, Orchard Houses, Forcing Beds, &c., are given.

**"CARDS."**
WHIST Hands illustrated by "Cavendish," with Notes on other Games.

Also Articles relating to "THE NATURALIST," "FOREIGN FIELD SPORTS," "RACQUETS," "BILLIARDS," &c., &c.

SUBSCRIPTION—Quarterly, 7s.; Half-Yearly, 14s.; Yearly, £1 8s

OFFICE: 346, STRAND, LONDON, W.C.

*Advertisements.*

# HIND'S

# ALTERATIVE PILLS
## FOR DOGS.

These Pills are offered to Breeders of Sporting and other Dogs as a safe and convenient remedy to have always on hand in case of sudden illness of their Animals. A dose given when the Dog first shows signs of Disorder generally puts him all right, and prevents the development of serious disease.

Being coated with Gelatine these Pills are rendered tasteless, consequently are easily administered, and are clean to handle. Their being quite tasteless is a great matter when we consider how easily a Dog can provoke himself to sickness.

It is not claimed for these Pills that they will cure every disease the Dog is heir to, but it is a well known fact that when the system is in a healthy state it offers a condition the least favourable to the development of disease, or in other words, it is almost proof against either Contagion or Infection. But it is claimed for the Pills, they keep a Dog in perfect health if given occasionally, or when he shows the least sign of being out of form; it is on this principle they have won such a wide reputation as a PREVENTIVE OF DISTEMPER.

Young Dogs are the most liable to an attack of Distemper during the period of Dentition, viz., from three to six months old (though they are frequently attacked by it up to eighteen months, but rarely after that age, unless of the malignant kind contracted at shows), and should during that period be very carefully watched; under any circumstances, a dose of the Pills should be given once a fortnight, but if the Dog should refuse its usual food, or appear at all out of sorts, a dose must be given at once, and repeated in two days, unless he is all right again. It is very important that all Dogs be housed in comfortable dry kennels, free from draught, but well ventilated, and in young ones this is a *sine quâ non* if you wish to rear them. These Pills are also most excellent for getting Dogs into show condition, and should be given at intervals of three or four days for about three doses. All Dogs should have a dose at once on returning from a show, it will cleanse the stomach and bowels, and cool the system generally. The Pills are recommended by Mr. W. W. Thompson, Mr. Ralph, Mr. G. Hall, Mr. Easton, Mr. R. B. Lee, and most of the leading collie breeders and exhibitors.

*For Puppies and Dogs under 14lb. in weight I make a special sized Pill, more convenient than cutting the full sized ones in two.*

**The 5s. and 2s. 6d. Boxes are sent Post Free, the smaller ones postage extra.**

HIND'S "FEVER POWDERS," for the cure of Distemper.—In Boxes, 1s. and 2s. 6d., post free.

JAUNDICE BALLS, invaluable.—In Boxes, 1s. and 2s. 6d., post free.
LOTION FOR MANGE, &c., &c.

## T. W. L. HIND, Chymist, Kendal.

*Advertisements.*

# BOULTON AND PAUL,
## NORWICH.
## PORTABLE DOG KENNELS
### WITH NEW SLIDING BENCH.

**Bed always dry.**

Regd. No. 30550.
*Registered Sliding Benches 5s., 7s. 6d., and 10s. 6d. extra. Troughs, 3s. each.*

These kennels are well made and highly finished. All parts are accessible for cleansing and disinfecting. The SLIDING BENCH is an important addition to the kennel, as it adds greatly to the comfort of the dog. They take to pieces and pack flat for travelling.

Reduced Cash Prices — Carriage Paid.

Fox Terriers, £1; for Colleys, Spaniels, or Retrievers, £1 15s.; for St. Bernards or Mastiffs, £2 15s.

## LEAN-TO KENNELS AND YARDS.
**REDUCED CASH PRICES.    CARRIAGE PAID.**

One House and Yard ... £7 10 0 | Two Houses and Yards £14 0 0

*Special Estimates given for Kennelling and Iron Railings.*

Every requisite for the KENNEL, POULTRY YARD, PHEASANTRY, AVIARY, &c., manufactured by ourselves.

**CAUTION** — Do not be misled by inferior imitations offered by unscrupulous people who copy our designs. We are the Original Manufacturers and Inventors of these specialities, which are made under practical supervision and by first-class workmen. All articles bear makers' name.

CATALOGUES FREE BY POST.

**BOULTON and PAUL, NORWICH.**
WE HAVE <u>NO AGENTS</u>.    PLEASE APPLY DIRECT.

*Advertisements.*

# £1000 FOR A COLLIE!

Mr. T. H. STRETCH,

whose sale for £1000 of the

## Collie "Christopher"

electrified the KENNEL World, writes:

"I always use Spratt's Distemper Powders, and find them most excellent."

**GIVE ON FIRST PREMONITORY SYMPTOMS.**

*Pamphlet on Canine Diseases Post Free.*

## SPRATT'S PATENT LIMITED,
LONDON, S.E.

www.ingramcontent.com/pod-product-compliance
Lightning Source LLC
Chambersburg PA
CBHW020831230426
43666CB00007B/1181